BARE NAKED

at the

REALITY DANCE

Journal One

Suzanne Selby Grenager

BAKULA
BOOKS

BAKULA BOOKS

920 Rosstown Road, Lewisberry, PA 17339

www.barenakedattherealitydance.com

Cover and interior design: Shannon Bodie, Lightbourne, Inc.

Library of Congress information is on file with the publisher.

ISBN 978-0-9836445-0-7

First Edition
Printed in the United States
10 9 8 7 6 5 4 3 2 1

BARE
NAKED
at the
REALITY
DANCE

For Lynn —
With much love
and all support
for listening to
your own dear
heart! Suzanne

Praise for

Bare Naked at the Reality Dance

"Suzanne Grenager writes with candor and grace in this beautiful, inspiring guide to finding the love within you, and using that love to transform your world."

—Jim Dreaver, author of *End Your Story, Begin Your Life:*
Wake Up, Let Go, Live Free and *The Way of Harmony*

"*Bare Naked at the Reality Dance* is a wise, deeply spiritual companion that invites reflection and is meant to be savored. This life-affirming journey buoys the reader through sharing experiences and feelings so personal and real they speak to us all. Reminiscent of Barry Stevens' Gestalt classic *Don't Push the River*, Suzanne's is a meatier, more inspirational achievement. She offers us something greater than her own rich ruminations and even than herself—not by giving answers from already enlightened heights like most spiritual books, but by inspiring readers to find their own."

—Mary Fowke, MA, Gestalt Therapist, Lisbon, Portugal

"What I most appreciate about Suzanne's work is how completely she's been able to shift my perspective, opening my awareness to what feels true inside. I hear her voice all the time, gently guiding me to see things as they are, not how my ego might want them to be. That's a lasting gift, which I urge you to give yourself by reading this book, where her understanding, illumination and support are alive on every page."

—Tom Moon, author of *1000 Recordings to Hear Before You Die*

"I wish I'd met Suzanne sooner but things come to us when we are ready. We think of readiness for adversity, but there must be readiness for bliss as well. Bliss is what Suzanne brings to me and the people she touches. It is very easy now for me to be mindful of every experience, receptive and thankful for those around me. It's as if I am somebody else. Suzanne has been the catalyst and I can't thank her enough for the bliss of freedom through awareness. If you are ready for bliss, read this book."

—Claudia Didia, MD, Assistant Professor of Medicine, El Paso, TX

"Bravo! In *Bare Naked at the Reality Dance*, Suzanne Grenager has dared to share her deepest self. As Margaret Wheatley suggests we must do in her groundbreaking book, *Finding Our Way: Leadership for an Uncertain Time*, Suzanne is willing to be disturbed and to partner with uncertainty and confusion, on her way to a larger life. Suzanne's spiritual journey is an inspiration to everyone who wants to give themselves permission to extend their reach and rise to greater heights. As an executive coach and coaching teacher, I was moved and informed by this compelling real-life story of self-exploration and transformation. As a woman with a story of my own, I chuckled and reveled in it right along with her."

—Pat Mathews, MA, RN, MCC, President of Mathews Associates, a coaching and consulting practice, and Program Director of the Leadership Coaching Program at Georgetown University

"Wow! *Bare Naked at the Reality Dance* is absolutely incredible. I love Suzanne's voice, so full of leadership and life. The personal stories, interwoven with her inspired practical wisdom, are intensely vulnerable, honest and powerful. I kept thinking, *Did she write this specifically for me?* because she so beautifully describes the way I feel. Many lives will be changed by this amazing woman and her generous offering of herself."

—Rachel Wilson, Owner of Om My Yoga, Senior Trainer for YogaFit Training Systems

For my Norwegian Prince of a husband, Trond, whose remarkable character, courage and kindness speak volumes all their own.

Honey, this is your book too!

Contents

Part III: Putting Myself First
November 2004

Part IV: Dancing with Bapu and Maha
November 2004 into January 2005

Part V: Bliss, Love and a Big "So What?"
January 2005

Part VI: Courage-Building, Cautionary Kripalu
January 2005

Part VII: A Confidence Born of Self-Care
January 2005

❧ ❧ ❧

Prologue

It was the luminous Carol Keller who showed me I am
the scribe and that this writing I do from deep in the
heart of me is not as I'd told her "just my journal." When
Carol showed up out of the blessed blue and asked to type
the words that kept on coming to me, we didn't know she
would be transformed beyond our wildest imaginings.
And it took me a while to understand what she'd said
from the start: that the words you will read are her words
and, we both now believe, *your* words as much as they are
mine, and that you may be as changed by reading them as
I was by writing them.

Carol and I worked together for months, I coaching
her and she typing up the writing I had been doing by hand
and wanted to preserve, if not yet sure why. But more than
the intense live coaching sessions about her life, it turned
out to be the words about my life that most stirred Carol
and helped her burgeon. More than anything, her dramatic
transformation is what led me to realize that it is my sacred
trust—my mission in this lifetime—to tell my story, in
order to mark the exhausting, exhilarating struggle for all
of us who have yearned to know ourselves as the Gods and
Goddesses incarnate we sense but don't quite realize we are.

It has become my job, I see and humbly accept, to
embody and record the raw everyday truths flowing through
the lives of aware people like you and me, people who

long and struggle to live from the stunning, life-altering awareness of who we are, the "I am that I am" we were born to. When I began to write in the big blank sketchbooks of my journal, I had only the barest glimmer of what was coming, the torrent of words and the role I've been groomed to play. I do not mean to make too much of it. But like many of us, I am in the habit of making too little of it, playing small out of the pervasive human fear of getting too big, or having others think I have. Well, I am done with that. I cannot encourage in you the greatness I do not see and allow to grow in me.

This book and the ones that will follow shape a collective story of the gradual, often painful coming-into-her-own of one particular woman. While this woman I am is still sometimes rife with fear and doubt, it's less and less, thank God—and thanks to decades of down-and-dirty personal growth work—*the more I am willing to be my outrageous self.* I now understand that my story is essentially your story, my inspiration, struggles and triumphs holding a universal mirror for the transformation we must all undergo if we are to save ourselves and our world from fear.

As always when fear is involved, the way out of our individual and collective calamity is to dive into the heart of our own dear selves, from where fear and love, and the war and peace they foment, spring. We must learn to love and trust ourselves, one success and misstep at a time. For until we uncover and claim the light in our individual hearts, the light of Mother Earth cannot shine forth again. I am here to help you do that, not my way, but in a way that is radically yours.

There is something else going on here, too, beyond the intimate, encouraging example of an awakened life lived at the edge. Mysterious as it is to me, the thundering-from-the-heart words in this book seem to carry a heady hit of powerful transformative energy. This energy, I believe, is what is drawing us mortals—inexorably, if we let it—from the unreal to the real, from darkness to light, and from death to immortality, as a saint I once knew (and whom you will get to know) used to say. It's a force that hit me often as I wrote the words you will read, and it almost swept Carol away.

Some call this sacred energy *Divine Mother Kundalini Shakti.* Shakti is an Indian Goddess who represents the universal source of the love and light we all essentially are. My years as a yoga teacher and disciple of an Indian guru predisposed me to the idea of strong inspirational energy as an Indian Goddess, though I can't say I've ever seen her except in the ubiquitous statues and drawings throughout India. Still, I daresay it is *Divine Mother,* a sacred feminine presence, who has been coming through to help me on my way, so I might help you on yours.

Shakti came to me, I suppose, because though I kicked and screamed and denied a lot along the way as you'll see, I allowed her to come. I was willing finally to face down my fear—of writing, of seeming to set myself up as a "spiritual teacher" and of showing up so large in the world that I could be shot down in a big way too. As you will also see, I learned to quiet my mind enough to attend to the signs and listen to my heart and gut, where divinity in whatever form manifests. I sat myself down to do what I came to do. And that is all I want for you—that you listen to *your* heart and gut, and risk living and loving from the terrifying edge where inner guidance leads you.

PART 1

Feet to the Fire
with Maha

August into October 2004

August 17, 2004

It's Time to Climb Again

I spend—make that *waste*—oodles of time doing ordinary things like drinking that wine of mine, eating meats, sweets and practically everything else but roadkill. I read cheesy magazines to "keep up." I watch TV and movies I could definitely do without. I get my hair cut and colored to look younger and prettier. I make up my aging face for public consumption for precisely that reason, and I shop (speaking of consumption) for the same *keeping up appearances* purpose. Most wasteful though is the fretting I do about it all.

Still, what's so wrong with that? Nothing is *wrong*, except unlike most people who do that and way worse, I've been knocked awake and trained by the best of them to be anything but ordinary: a spiritual scribe, if I daresay it. Yes. A spiritual scribe is who I am and what I am meant to be. When I stop to remember, I know it like my many names. There is no excuse but fear to keep me from living my destiny. *Thy will be done, oh Lord, not mine.*

Now that I see I have been hiding out under the mantle of ordinary—as if I didn't know who I am and what I am meant to be up to—the trick is not to *hate* myself for it. The trickier trick is to let the new awareness transform me. Must I fall apart and wallow in shame, or writhe in physical pain, as I've often done before in the interest of personal growth and transformation?

Maybe. Or just maybe I can instead say yes to the query my soon-to-be life coach Maha recently posed for me: *Are you ready to grow without pain?* What a great question! And God knows I'd like to be. So here's what *I* want to know: Is it time to pick myself up and make my way—gently this time—over the next ridge? Might I be able to move toward expansive views and heightened awareness without going to hell and back every other step of the way?

I have traveled too far to go back, and I know too much to forget, two resonant clichés that present two more simple questions for me: *Where am I? What do I know?*

I am at the further reaches of the plateau I've been walking for a while. Standing still is not an option, though I sure wish it were. What I know is it's time to climb again— with renewed patience and greater surrender and trust. I must ask for and be open to receive all the help I can get.

I must remember that however lonely I sometimes feel, I am not alone, and that grace is a state we don't have to *earn*, not in the usual sense of the word, tit for tat.

Grace is a state we don't have to earn, not in the usual sense of the word, tit for tat.

Grace happens when we waltz our cumbersome minds out of the way of the heart and soul. Grace is re-*membering*, embodying again in our members, the knowledge we are born with and forget—that *I am The Way, The Truth and The Life.* I am that, for where else would wisdom reside but in the divinely inspired beings that I am and you are? When we abide in the pure awareness that is grace, we know that *we are the one we have been waiting for.*

Are these mere words I write, or are they transmissions of truth? Are they grace come to life on the page? I do not know for sure. I do know I resonated with the sweet words of Eckhart Tolle's *Stillness Speaks* earlier this morning. And now it's my own words creating in me a cosmic pulsation. Our words, his and mine, have the power to move us because they are not *his* words and *my* words. The words we write from our hearts are *our* words—whether Tolle's, mine or yours. What comes through me now is not by or for me alone; it is a universal expression, the sum total of humankind thrumming to the wordless harmony we call life.

Ego cannot understand these heartfelt words of ours. All it knows to do is wordlessly grasp, and grasp some more. It is ever fearful that it won't get what it wants, or that it will get what it doesn't want, and will be miserable either way. Ego knows only the words it's been told and has taken to heart—a pack of heartbreaking lies. We live our lives for those lies, and our hearts *are* broken.

They are broken, but they are not broken *open*, which would bring us everything the lies promise but do not deliver, and so much more. No, our hearts are *broken*, as in crippled, stunted, diseased and useless, anything but open. We know nothing of love—*agape*— the only thing we have ever wanted.

We know nothing of love — agape — the only thing we have ever wanted.

wanted. What a sorry state of affairs! Yes, I see that is where I am and where we are, the sad wide world of us. Now for how to fix it, that broken heart of *mine* first off.

August 20, 2004

If I Were Bapuji

It's the day before my son—Trond's and mine—was born thirty-three years ago. I will not live that long again. *So much to do, so little time,* quips my mind as if to goad me on. But I won't be goaded. The weather changed yesterday from soft summer sky and 80 degrees to dark, gloomy and cold. Here in our Nova Scotia summer cottage, I am bundled up and hunkered down against the rain, fog, chill, and that goading mind of mine. With Trond gone back to Pennsylvania to tend to business, I'm here alone all week and feeling anxious.

Yesterday, I felt better for a bit, thanks to calls with two of my life coaching clients, where I got to bring much of who I am to bear. I was bolstered, too, by the prospect of a massage, which turned into a session of deep painful shoulder work. The idea was to get at the ingrained tensions that have lately held my poor neck stiff as a proverbial board. It was not a "feel good" massage, nor meant to be. Nor is this latest Nova Scotia masseuse of mine the gifted healer Kim Beckett is, she who used to hold and love me like an angel.

Oh, God, how can I do that for myself? How, please, can I pick up the abandoned child inside, hold her close and roll her back into the heart? *So much to do, so little time,* methinks again. The inner fog persists and I am unclear about what is mine to do with the shrinking time I have left. Okay, it's to *bring more love,* I know it, but how to do that gently and effectively. How, please, do I spread love around—or better yet, awaken it in others' hearts, as my blessed Bapuji did?

Bapuji kept silence, meditated ceaselessly, and wrote. He had no family or ordinary life like mine. People gave him shelter and brought him food. There was nothing he had to do but pray, and even that was his choice. If I would be like Bapuji, and I'd like to be, I've got a challenge—the package I am wrapped in, a very different disguise from a swami's saffron robes.

Bapuji, which means beloved Grandfather, was the nickname for Swami Kripalvananda, for whom the Kripalu Yoga that I practiced and taught for many years was named. Bapuji came to America from India in 1977 to bestow his blessings on his spiritual grandchildren at the Kripalu Center, then located in my state of Pennsylvania. So I was often in his presence during the four-and-a-quarter years he surprised us all by staying. And I was far more affected by him than I realized until I began turning my journal into a book and found his wise, loving influence throughout.

❖ ❖ ❖

But the American Girl is a disguise of sorts, too, a persona embodying the sadhak yogini and scribe beneath.

This journal writing is starting to feel truer than any other way I know to share the awareness growing wild in me, and with it, Bapuji's love. What better means than this direct and simple one to inspire those who know they are looking for love but look in all the wrong places—outside themselves. How better than this humble diary medium to kick-start disgruntled souls who know something is not right but, like me once (and *still* sometimes), haven't a clue what's the matter.

I read some of this recent writing aloud to my original life coach Kimberly, and to my soon-to-be new one, Maha. I found myself moved by the spare truth I've laid down on the page, which they both told me moved them too. I've been putting pen to the great white void of this black sketchbook without much thought or effort these days, the words arriving in the same easy out-of-the-blue way my poems came in the year 2000—as naked, unimpeded wisdom from the heart.

The American-Girl-in-Canada hears a knock on the cottage door. If I were Bapuji, it would be a disciple bringing me breakfast. But no, when I put down my pen and get up to answer the door, I see it's our carpenter friend and neighbor Pat and his painter sidekick, here in Trond's absence for a consult with me about finishing the floor of the guest loft above the new garage.

We look at samples, we make a plan. They thank me and leave, returning me reluctantly to the page. But it is no longer the act of writing itself (which used to terrify me), or even the frequent householder interruptions, that tests me most. The bigger challenge has been to see if I can write in a way that feels right for public consumption, though I'm not sure that's it either. *Am* I to write for public consumption? Who says? My ego for sure, though lately my heart has chimed in. My greatest challenge may be simply to sit myself down consistently to write what feels right for me.

I've never been much for discipline, so years ago when Bapuji offered us *surrender* I glommed onto it like a baby bird to its mommy's worm. "Love, service and *surrender*"

> **Surrender** is a spiritual concept having little to do with the white flag of defeat. The antidote to making life happen from willful mind, surrender is about letting life happen through the heart. In Christian parlance, surrender is alive in the words, "Thy will be done, Oh Lord, not mine."
>
> ❧ ❧ ❧

was his motto and his mantra. It summed up the way he lived and the values he encouraged us seekers to embrace.

Maha believes far more in discipline than I've cared—or is it *dared?*—to do. But is my stout defense of surrender over her practice of will simply a reactionary response on my part? No doubt I am anti-authoritarian: *I want to do what I want to do, and not what I don't.* It's the refrain of a rebellious little girl who was not the one her parents ordered, knew deep down she never would be, and didn't like trying to meet their expectations one bit. Is Maha my new Mommy? Maybe, but even if the seditious child has kicked in here, mightn't it be okay, maybe best, for me to do only what I want to do?

Discipline isn't an issue when we do what we love to do. But I need to know what that is. *Is* it to share my writing more widely? If *Discipline isn't an issue when we do what we love to do.* so, which writing are we talking about? And might I have to discipline myself to do it? Possibly not. The journal words, which speak from the heart to the heart—like Bapuji's life and presence, I hope—flow as naturally as my breath. Little *discipline* needed. The words come through me from heart to hand to pen to page with ease and, yes, grace. It *is what it is* and whatever *it* is, I feel it changing me in ways my calculated writing never has.

Unlike individual articles about something I have done or known, or the memoir I started, which rehashed and tried to make sense of the past, this writing makes sense of the here and the now, as it happens; it helps me face the emotional challenges of this moment, turning my fear back to love today. When I start with what's up for me personally in this minute, I seem to move naturally from my particular situation to what feel like larger life lessons, rife with universal truths for us all.

I started this regular journal-writing practice to bring the clarity, emotional resolution and peace of mind that keep me grounded in myself. Both kinds of writing, the journal by hand I do for me and the stories on the computer that I composed with a reader in mind, may add to my store of wisdom, and the larger world's. But this journaling, which feels almost like *transmission*, is more organic and compelling by far. How these two types of writing might come together to create the book I have long meant to write—perhaps along with my poems— remains a wide open question.

If Maha can help me think this through, she will be of invaluable service. Now I am off to read her "Welcome to Life Coaching" materials in advance of our first official call.

> **Life coaching** is a service that helps people clarify their values, appreciate their strengths and align their lives with who they most essentially are. After my multi-faceted career as a teacher, writer, yoga instructor, mentor and body-mind therapist, life coaching seemed like a natural follow-on, bringing all of me to bear as it does. I love that the work is over the phone, leveling the playing field. And I love its premise that clients know best how to create a life of fulfillment and joy uniquely their own. Unlike traditional therapy, which explores what's wrong, goes back and asks *why*, coaching builds on what's right, urges clients forward and asks *why not*.
>
> ❧ ❧ ❧

August 24, 2004

A House Divided

L ife is a great festival and I am an honored guest. I remember that most mornings, so long as I sit still reading words that encourage gratitude and equanimity. I gaze out the trio of floor-to-ceiling windows in our living room and am treated to a panoramic view of Mill Cove and sky. It looks like a big three-panel Georgia O'Keefe cloud *oeuvre* I once saw. A massive mottled rock anchors my view in the middle of the center window, but *I*, I notice, am not anchored in my middle.

A gull catches the wind and sails across the soft blue canvas peopled with pale gray clouds, which slowly threaten to overtake and fill it. A great green tree framing my view on the left shakes its multitude of leaves for a minute and then goes still as a painting. It's another beautiful Nova Scotia morning, and I am still here alone, and in a way not here and not entirely alone.

Again this morning I am a house invaded and divided by my mind, and I am sick of it. The rude machinations of my head are keeping me from the wholeness of my heart. While I am wise enough to know that none of this is me—and that *all* of it is—I continue to choose suffering.

This is not serious suffering we are talking about, but a low-grade insipid malaise I apparently enjoy being stuck in. Ever since Trond left to return to Pennsylvania, I've felt abandoned, not by him, but by me. I am angry and disappointed I am not doing more—in his absence and in general—to share myself and my presumed gifts, as a writer, teacher and inspirational force, with the larger world in need of love. Isn't it about time?

A nano-second later, I am flooded with doubt about what I have to offer anyway. "Who do you think you are?" my ego taunts me. How can you presume to be an example to others when you are such a mess yourself? Let Tolle and Byron Katie, who seem freer by far, be the teachers. Where has your so-called pathless path gotten you that you should dare to share it with the wide world?

> **Byron Katie**, the author of *Loving What Is*, developed a radical process called The Work. It involves asking ourselves four questions about anyone or anything we judge or find difficult. Her truth-baring practice inevitably has us turning the spotlight back on the self to discover the source of the problem within. Katie's process has inspired my coaching and personal growth work.
>
> ❧ ❧ ❧

Okay, ego, you are right—I've been undone this week, and not exactly willing to do what needs to be done to undo my undoneness. That, my path suggests, is to be *in it, with it, okay with it*, letting myself come as undone as God would have me do. How does that work? You stop getting in your way, Suzanne. You let go of any agenda but *being here now* and *loving what is*—thank you, Tolle and Katie. And thank *you*, Suzanne, for stopping to remember what you, too, know.

A fat brown-striped kitty strides into view through the living room window, crossing our deck for a sec before just as quickly disappearing. I smile. But *sans* the distraction, the twinge in my colon and tightness around my heart, which I've felt all morning, are right back at me. I take a quick, deep breath in, and let it out with a sigh…. Okay, there's a little more life in you now, girl.

I begin to move out of my head, where stuckness starts and stays, breathing a sallow, shallow life of its own. But along with paying attention, this writing about what I notice is a way to work with it, to reclaim the heart by dropping (or lifting) me into the so-called Higher Self, where there is compassion for the so-called lower one—the poor, egoic part of us. I love to write this way, *and* I don't want to give up my dream of writing a real book. Maybe I don't have to. It has been suggested—even, we know, by me to myself in a bold moment—that rather than trying to write *a magnum opus*, I locate someone to type up these handwritten notes and make *them* into a book.

God is a term I seem to use interchangeably with life, reality, Source, the universe, love, and the Self of All (the latter also my synonym for what some call the non-egoic soulful Higher Self). God is the word that slips out when I feel particularly inspired by life's mystery. Do I *believe in God*? I don't know. Maybe, since the God word has shown up often during this writing I let flow.

❖ ❖ ❖

Scary as it is, that idea causes less churning in my stomach than the thought of turning articles I've written into proper chapters, writing more of them, and organizing it all into a proper tome. That means something too. But it all feels hard at the moment, and I know hard is never what's needed. Soft, easy, peaceful, *surrendered*, is always, in all ways, the way. Why the fuck can't I live it?

Ah, but hear the violence, the hardness of heart toward yourself, my dear, in that angry F-worded question. Oh, dear God, why are we so hard on ourselves—and we nearly all are. Why can't we more easily see that our intentions are good, as God knows they are, when we are conscious

enough to have intentions at all? We must learn to trust that
we are doing our best, a courtesy we grant even strangers
who screw up. We must
let up on ourselves a bit;
we must.

> *We must learn to trust that we are doing our best, a courtesy we grant even strangers who screw up.*

I'm beginning to see
I must be willing to be
precisely where I am,
however *hard*, before I
am free to be anywhere else. Surrender—not striving—
brings transcendence. If we are not to stay stuck, we must
be willing to feel the pain, the exact physical sensations
and psychic consequences we've brought on ourselves by
choosing strife over surrender. The practice becomes to let
life come—everything we perceive within and without—
and then, as best we can, to let it go. We can't let go what
we haven't let come. We must receive our dear life without
holding on for dear life.

I want to be of greater service, I honestly do. Please
show me how. Let this morning's coaching call with Maha
bring me closer to myself and to what is and is not mine to
do and share.

Thy will be done, Oh Lord, not mine.

August 25, 2004

A House United Again

When we live in and from our minds, there is bound to be at least low-level tension, because the *I* that is our mental awareness of ourselves is not lined up with the *I* that is our body. The body is always here *now*, and if we live in the mind, our awareness is in the past or in the future. Mind is the province of dreams and memories (along with figuring out stuff, which creates a tension all its own). But to the extent we are thinking about anything at all, we are not fully present in our bodies, which creates the tension of separation. We are a *house divided*—body from mind—and nobody is home.

For as it's famously said, home is where the heart is, and when we live in our heads, we are heartless, homeless, lost. We think our thoughts, speak our words and decide to act without being informed by Source, the truth and love that we are. Lacking our inner compass, we miss the point, the very reason for our existence—to love and be loved from and for *all* of who we are. We think we are supposed to do something brilliant out there, when all we really need to do is bask in our innate brilliance.

We think we are supposed to do something brilliant out there, when all we really need to do is bask in our innate brilliance.

Jesus got it right, even if many who took his name did not. He said: *I am the light of the world*, and there's every reason to think that is also our destiny, yours and mine. For when I drop out of my head into the heady, holy terrain of the heart, there can be no difference between who I am and who Christ was and is. We are all cut from the same divine cloth, sweet relics of the God who made us and who would have us return as simple supplicants to his holy lotus feet.

I only know these truthful things (if often dimly) when I suspend thought. And that, it turns out, is both all the discipline we need, and for some of us, the hardest thing in the world to do. The trick is to stop the mind, stunning her into sweet stillness before she knows what's hit her.

The phrase "**holy lotus feet**" is part and parcel of the path of yoga, with its gurus and disciples. Bowing down to and even kissing the guru's feet, which are said to be as pure and fruitful as the thousand-petalled lotus flower, is an act of reverence for a yoga devotee. In this way, the disciple puts her head below her heart, symbolizing (and ultimately realizing) a surrender of her will to the higher good the guru represents. For me, the term is synonymous with humility and love.

❧ ❧ ❧

That's what I do first thing in the morning here in Nova Scotia while Trond is away. I get up, change out of my pajamas or not, and quickly fix my ritual black tea with cream and honey. Settling into the old blue and vanilla striped couch we brought here from the farm, I gaze down at the rippling waters of Mill Cove and out across the gray rocks. I close my eyes, letting the call of a gull, now the wail of a neighbor's bagpipe, creep in past my mind and return me to inner stillness.

It is remarkably quiet when birds and bagpipe suddenly stop. But it's a vibrant silence, which overcomes me in waves, until I rest in it and it in me. When I set it up like this, full of intention to get ahead and ahold of my mind before it can get ahold of me—when I do what that takes, which is just about nothing *but* intend—nothing bothers me. Even a phone call from Trond, in Maine making his way north, does not interrupt the palpable flow of peace to and from my heart.

I find myself taking big deep gulps of air now, as if to ground me in this often elusive clarity of mind and fullness of heart. I could sit here all day like this. But I can't, which is to say I won't, because I have an agenda, beginning with an exercise regimen before my coaching call in an hour. Will I maintain the peace while I strengthen my muscles and talk with a client? More importantly, can I accept myself and what arises if I don't? Yes and yes again, so long as I stay connected with that Source we call heart, through the power of Divine Mother's breath.

The concept of **Divine Mother** exists side by side in some spiritual traditions with the idea of a Holy Father. The concept is central to Hinduism, which is closely related to the path of Kripalu Yoga I followed for almost two decades during the 1970s and '80s. For me, Divine Mother represents a powerful feminine energy, which can be awakened and enhanced through deep yoga breathing, known as pranayama, my most enduring and consistent spiritual practice.

❖ ❖ ❖

September 2, 2004

Hiding Out in My Family No More

Well, it's a whole other day in my once drowsy inner and outer worlds. And to kick things off, here come the clichés: There is no rest for the weary once the happily napping cat is out of the bag—the *weary* in this case being yours truly, and the *cat* being my consciousness. Once we have been awakened, we cannot so successfully fall asleep again, not without a drug habit or other serious addiction; and even then, likely not for long. And awakened I have been, again!

Here I was in sleepy Chester, Nova Scotia, my ego hoping for a vacation of sorts—after all it is summer and we are by the sea—and what do I do? I up and hire a bell-ringer to keep me *up and at it*, week after week after week. And she's good, this one, dangerously good (says my nervous ego). I am talking, of course, about my new life coach Maha.

We had our third phone session yesterday, despite a not-so-clever ploy on my part to avoid it. With Trond back from Pennsylvania, Nora here for her summer visit, and her boyfriend Jack plus Sam and Kayda all on their way, I tried to get myself off the hook, asking Maha if we might postpone the last two of the four coaching calls I'd agreed to. *Couldn't we just wait till everybody went home?*

Not if Maha had anything to say about it, we couldn't. As I feared, Maha caught me in the act of avoidance, saying I am hiding, presumably from myself—and as she bluntly put it, from the work I am here to do. We both know that isn't about entertaining myself or the family. No, it is soul work: the evolutionary, transformational business of freeing this sometime lost soul of mine from the sticky web of doubts and fears in which it has long been enmeshed.

I've heard tell the longing to be free must be paramount in order to be realized—for us spiritual seekers to be realized. What I see, thanks to Maha, is that *long* as I might, I do not yet long enough. Maha and I agreed on an earlier call that I am dulling myself with drink, and now she shows me I am hiding from myself and my soul work right in the bosom of my family. Oh, God!

Much as I hate to admit it, Maha is right. The yogic scriptures are very clear on this point. If we are to be free and to know God as ourselves, we must be willing to sacrifice everything that is *not* that—*everything*. We may never *have* to renounce it all, but we'd better be ready and willing to. "Give up even thy soul to him," says the authoritative *Sri Guru Gita*, with not a shred of ambiguity.

Lest we miss the point, the same scripture instructs: "Wife or husband thou must release;" the seeker is urged to look way past the family for sustenance. It doesn't mean we must get divorced or retreat to a cave. It means God and guru—and so, the self—are to be honored above all else.

The *Sri Guru Gita*, or "Song of the Guru," has long been my favorite Yogic scripture. I listened to and sang along with a taped English version of it countless mornings over many years. If yoga breathing has been my most enduring yoga practice, chanting the *Sri Guru Gita* was the most inspirational, thanks to its promise of countless blessings, and its heart-opening devotional tone.

❖ ❖ ❖

I know there is no other way but to be willing to let everything go—and I can hardly bear it. Tears well up, as I comprehend what Maha, in all her fierce courage, is exhorting me to do. "When will you start saying no?" she asked me, and my entire arsenal of defenses rose up as one. "I *do* say no; I have *great* boundaries," I insisted at first. But even as those words arose in my head, I knew, from the place in my heart that once awakened never sleeps, she spoke the truth: I sell myself and my purpose short, day in, day out, in myriad ways, small and not so small after all.

"Thy will be done, Oh Lord, not mine" is easy to say and to feel as a possibility, while meditating and journaling like this. But to *live* sweet surrender to the soul, in the thick of family life, here, now, in a teensy cottage, overrun however thoughtfully with Trond, Nora, and her much adored dog Delilah playing with her lobster squeaky toy on the other side of a thin wall, that is a challenge—and one I am thankfully starting to see my way through, for the moment if not beyond.

Yep, Maha has shown up to show me that I betray myself. By asking to postpone our calls, which represent my current commitment to my life's purpose, I relegated my soul to the back burner. It's one glaring example of how willing I've been to find convenient excuses to abandon myself, and forgo my journey to restore *me* to my rightful place on the throne of my heart.

However casual I wanted it to be, I made a solemn commitment, to Maha and to myself, to show up on the phone for coaching every week this month. Now I wanted out, precisely of course because I need practice in staying the course of commitment—to myself, to others, and to God.

Being here writing right this moment is a step toward honoring that commitment. This is sacred time I make for my heart's desires and the chance to speak them on the page. The easy thing to do this morning—what I would have done without Maha's reminders—was to go out and chat with Nora (who just came over from her guest quarters), as any ordinary mother who loves her daughter dearly would do. Trond has been in and out of the cottage, too. I love them both very much, but morning is my holy time. And *I want to do this,* this thing that feeds me and my soul.

This is sacred time I make for my heart's desires and the chance to speak them on the page.

You have a pattern of hiding out in your family. When are you going to say no?

It was with Maha's words ringing in my head—and my heart chiming in—that I excused and recused myself as soon as Nora showed up. After a quick hello, I was back in the relative haven of this little room of mine. I closed the door behind me and sat down on the bed to write. When Nora and Trond got noisy, I popped in earplugs. When I was distracted by Nora throwing balls for Delilah right outside the window I face (where else?), I drew the blinds. There is now a riotous lot of coming and going through the front door just outside my room. Tempted as I've been to give up—if you can't beat 'em, join 'em!—I'm resisting, and getting stronger by the minute as I do.

So this is what commitment looks like. It feels as right as it does strange, to sit here in splendid isolation, tending to me first while my family swirls around in a nearby sphere. I know it might sound selfish and crazy. But Maha is right: I matter too much not to start saying "no" to soul work distractions. *Thy will be done, Oh Lord, not mine,* and give me the wisdom to know the difference. *Good for me* for letting the truth in Maha's words resonate with the truth in my soul.

The inquiry I created for myself at the end of the coaching call I didn't get out of is this: *How can I be true to myself no matter what?* The challenge posed by this question is sure to get even tougher in the next few days, with the arrival of Jack, Sam and Kayda. What I want to do is hold that intention as steadily as I'd hold a meditative gaze upon a flame. I must intend to be true and I must be willing to let go and (as they say) *let God.* Thank you, God; thank you, Maha, and thanks again to me too, for my willingness to keep looking through the daunting darkness for light.

September 4, 2004

Growth without Pain

When we started working together, Maha asked me if I was ready to grow without pain. Though we know I liked the question, I didn't fully get why she was choosing to ask me that, or exactly what she meant, though I had an inkling. Pain is part of life. And for the last three decades, I've tried my best to use angst, which arises when I resist what is, as a tool for the growth of my spirit.

"No pain, no gain" is a familiar litany on the field of sports—and of spiritual development. But I've never believed it. At first, when Lucy's death threw me into psychic pain beyond my wildest imaginings, I wasn't *trying* to use pain to grow. That is simply what happened. My choice to head for Sloan Kettering Cancer Center in 1975 to bear witness to the hideous demise of my oldest dear friend provoked a profound emotional tumult that unwittingly set me on my spiritual path.

The path I chose—or that chose me, which is how it felt— began with Kripalu Yoga, a tool for personal growth if there ever was one. During the first murderous months after losing Lucy, I learned that the dynamic duo of emotional pain and yoga was one hell of a vehicle for a freedom ride, though I didn't yet know the half of it. Over two decades of practicing and teaching yoga, doing the related body-mind work called the Rubenfeld Synergy Method, and plain sitting and squirming in pain, I have gotten better (and better than most, I dare say) at transmuting the challenging experience of fear— and sometimes sheer terror— back to Source love.

❖ ❖ ❖

I've often done the work, but I've also been stubborn about not doing it. As recently as the last two weeks when Trond was gone, there were times I failed to sit often enough with my angst to turn myself around. That is until Maha and her piercing questions provoked me. Today, a few weeks after she first asked me about growing without pain, I may better understand the question.

What she was asking, I think, is whether I might be willing and able to *choose the challenge of growth,* rather than having to be prompted or forced to it by the presence of unwanted psychic—or physical—irritation. Must I wait for fear, shame or pain to drive me back to myself, the loving Source I always am; or can I really decide to take growthful leaps in that direction when I am well and more or less happy? Might I elect the effort of expansion over complacency while nestled (but not hiding out) in the bosom of my family, in the thick of a full and fulfilling life?

Can I remember to do what it takes to stay self-connected then? After another day or so of shutting my door and putting my soul work first, the answer to Maha's question, I am thrilled to report, is yes. It is the same resounding "yes" she was asking for in my commitment to our work.

Thank you, dear Maha, for showing me I do not have to sacrifice one iota of the self-love and care that promote growth. I need not show my true self the door just because life's everyday demands—or other people—show up at my door. I can decide to put myself first without the benefit of even a minor

I need not show my true self the door just because life's everyday demands — or other people — show up at my door.

28

physical or spiritual emergency, and in the midst of a busy life.

The day before yesterday I had four long calls with coaching clients and still created space to sit, feel, and write the last lengthy entry here. Fully booked as I was, I made time for me and my journaling, which made my day. And the well-being I generated by choosing to put myself and my deepest needs first has lasted all through yesterday and into today. The used-to-be hard-won sense that I, sweet soul, am *enough* is with me even now, as I sit alone in the rain, looking forward to a not-so-thrilling day of laundry, housework and grocery shopping.

This gift of myself came to me not through pain. It came to me because I remembered and decided again that there is nothing in this world so precious as maintaining the deepest possible connection to my soul. There is nothing else, *nothing* that feeds me like this quiet joy, this peace that passes all understanding, this embrace of the One that I am, and that we all essentially are.

There is nothing in this world so precious as maintaining the deepest possible connection to my soul.

Self-transcendence is more dear to me, truly, than husband, children, probably life itself. At last the longing has grown great, and there is no time to waste. I must not and will not let anything tear me away again. That is my sacred intention, shared yesterday with my first (mentor) coach and friend Kimberly. She understands and is glad for me—and for herself, eager as she is to examine her own behavior in this new light that has been shed for us by Maha, and to continue the conversation she and I are also now engaged in—about how we can grow without pain.

Tomorrow is the day my not-so-little brother Sam and sister-in-law Kayda finally arrive, presenting a fresh challenge to my commitment to stay true to myself and to keep writing, even at the risk of offending them, which I dearly don't want to do. Whether in pain or joy, *en famille* or *toute seule*, no matter what the external circumstances, I'm going to try to be true.

I can grow in love without the prompt of fear. I've done it for forty-eight hours, using yoga, mantra, meditation, pranayama and mundane mind to keep returning me to myself. What is new, inspiring and potentially transformative is that I realize far more keenly now that the power is mine to choose self-nurturance always. Like never before, I understand how critical it is to remember to do it. I have long had the tools; now I better appreciate that I can use them in all situations. *Thy will be done, Oh Lord, not mine.* Yes indeed, thank God and everyone involved.

September 13, 2004

A Yogi's Way

Fall is in the air here in Nova Scotia, where I am now alone after a deluge of guests and nonstop socializing that would once have sunk me. Although I withdrew a little into a protective shell, I did my best not to hide out either in or from the family or from myself. And I did not drown. But with all the comings and goings, and the giving over of our bedroom loft and our not-quite-completed garage guest quarters—to Sam and Kayda, and Nora and Jack, respectively—there was very little time in my life, or room in our mini-compound, to be fully attentive to the Self of All that I am. That is not an excuse I hope, but an observation, which serves to remind me of the critical importance of creating the rest of my life as *sacred space* whenever and wherever I can.

But what do I mean by *sacred space*, which is the phrase that came to me in the way words do only when I am in sacred space. I mean if I am to value myself—my soul's vessel—in ways that serve me and the world around me, I must be attentive to the task of conserving my energy, from the inside out, and vice versa. I must protect myself from all influences that rob me of my spirit. As Maha understood and suggested, I *must choose to say no to everything but inspiration.*

Wow. That's a big one. Why? Because it requires I be consistently conscious—*vigilant*—about how what I do, say, think and feel *affects me.* And once I've got that straight, I would have to discipline myself to do only what lifts me up and not what brings me down. I said "Wow" because I got right away how different my life would look if I followed that newly minted guidance. It would look different on the outside, sure. But if I said no to everything but inspiration, I would instantly reap a quiet joy, contentment and peace on the inside, where it most matters.

But first, how might life be different outside? Well, as we've suggested before, I would finally spend—make that *waste* again!—less time watching videos and reading *Time*, *The New Yorker* and other stuff not pointing me to God. I might even cancel my *What Is Enlightenment?* magazine, which I sometimes find off-puttingly intellectual, its profiles of spiritual seekers and descriptions of spiritual tools rarely aflame with the heart-driven inspiration I need for walking a path of love.

Then there's Bapuji. Last night I began reading spontaneously to Trond from *Pilgrim of Love*. It's a book about Bapuji compiled by a Kripalu sister disciple, Atma Jo Ann Levitt. Sharing Bapuji stories aloud—stories about and stories told by him—I felt him come alive again. For me, Bapuji stands head and shoulders above everyone as a model of love incarnate. *He is who I would be.*

To live love and let everything else *go*: that was Bapuji's path, and it is my challenge. To let heart reign at the expense of whatever may stand in the way, including even my good name. Yep, I must let go of whatever may be left of my mistaken identity, my *reputation*—the way I have wished to be seen in my mother's, and last week my brother's, and always others' eyes. All that must go.

Of course little Suzie still wants to be loved. But the way to love is never through self (or self-image) protection, any more than it is through seeking love from outside. The way to love is direct. Love thyself and—by absolute extension—you will love your neighbor, and vice versa of course, whichever opportunity for love happens to present itself first. The way to love is love.

You learn this love, if you are lucky enough to have a lick of devotion, as I do, by giving yourself to God, to life, to yourself, to others, to whatever draws you, any way you can. Chant and dance if you dare. Kiss the ground or the guru's feet, or your dog's wet, sloppy face. Listen to heart-rending music, read scriptures or poetry or whatever words carry your mind to the deeper reaches of your heart, where love lives. Tend to lepers as Mother Teresa did. Walk in the woods, disappear among the trees. Let God have you always, in everything you do.

> **"Little Suzie"** is the name I gave to the "Inner Child." While training to become certified in the body-mind Rubenfeld Synergy Method, I discovered the little girl I once was buried deep inside, alive but not entirely well. I came to realize that, buried though she may be, "Little Suzie" was a force to be reckoned with—best, by loving her to death, as most parents seem unable to do.
>
> ❧ ❧ ❧

God realization is the answer, heart's love the quickest way. So why do we avoid it like the plague? Because it is so much easier to hide out in the mind, letting ego drug and drag us, dropping us anywhere but here, now, where heart prevails. It's far simpler to merge with the crowd at the trough of business as usual, to lose ourselves in our material girl (or guy)—to worship Madonna rather than the Christ Child of the heart—because we can almost pull it off; it's *what people do*, and we want desperately to fit in, feel good and get on with pulling off normal.

But I can't do normal so well any more. I leaf through

those magazines Trond thoughtfully brought back from his trip to Pennsylvania. The well-crafted rhetoric seems empty, when I am even able to pay attention. The news of ugly, ignorant, fear-driven political and personal behavior curdles the sweet milk of love that is my Source. Even my nightly hit of wine can feel sadly dulling now. Once you taste the real nectar again, it's hard to fall for pale imitations.

Once you taste the real nectar again, it's hard to fall for pale imitations.

I don't pretend to have a passion for God akin to Bapuji's. *All* he seemed to do was practice love, in his meditation, reading, writing, and sitting with us. But the more I taste divine nectar—the Sanskrit word is *amrit* (my once-guru's given name)—the more enticed I am. Love breeds love. Every act of true self-love, like writing my heart out in this journal, quickens the love in me *for* love, bringing me closer to myself, and so to everyone. Love works like that, thank God.

Bapuji must have been addicted to love. He himself said he "could not live a minute without it." How natural and how utterly abnormal to *love* love so much. Though everyone wants nothing more or less than love, most of us have gone so far afield in our search for it that Bapuji's one-pointed devotion to it stands practically alone, at least among those I've known, or known of.

I am not ready to retreat to a cave, stop speaking for years as he did, or meditate for hours on end, as a few folks I know say they do. But I want more God, more love, and more of the stillness and surrender that point the way. That must mean I want less of everything else. I must want to meditate more, do yoga again, and retreat further from the world in whatever ways I feel I can (or dare). I am lucky and grateful to live in two quiet places with an understanding family and the relative freedom to say no to much of the craziness that passes for normal on Planet Earth.

But if I am to be a beacon, I must somehow turn up the heat. I must stoke body and mind with the fire of my heart's desire, fueling its inborn capacity to love and be loved. I must go sailing with Trond, and let him make love to me, and make love back. I must wake up to what love does and does not look like, recognizing its myriad forms in a Western woman householder's daily drill.

I must make ongoing adjustments as I stay vigilant to what does and doesn't quicken my heart. As I once wrote in a poem, "love is what happens when there is nothing else going on." It slips in the door when we give up pushing against it or grappling for it (and for and against life itself). That must be why the yogic scriptures say: "When you can surrender in full love to God, you'll rise to the heights of the heaven within. In blissful awakening you'll know your true self, and fathom the depths of the whole universe." Devotional surrender is the most direct path to God, period.

Happily, we really can encourage love through whatever devotional practice we like; there is no one exclusive way. We can best let go into love by making everything devotional practice. We can stay connected to our source in the heart, and make that the business, the purpose, the mission of our every day, and little by little of our whole life. What on earth else is there to do?

So help me please to stop, breathe and re-*member*— literally breathing life and love back into my members again—as often as I can and must. That is a yogi's way.

October 7, 2004

Strange Dreams

Yesterday, I went for my first chiropractic session with Liz's chiropractor, Rory. The work he did, if you could call it that, was beyond subtle. It was nothing like the usual clicking and cracking I know as "chiropractic." But whew! The effects of a little finger tweak here at the neck, and a gentle placement of the hand there at the sacrum, have proven profound, as Rory warned.

I did a bunch of errands following the session. By the time I got home, I felt so weak, tired and sore I had to lie down on the couch for the rest of the day and let Trond wait on me. I headed for bed early, where I proceeded to sleep for an uncharacteristic ten hours. The long night was punctuated with wild vivid dreams, as Rory had promised. In the first, I was colonized by a succession of creatures from small bugs to big wild cats. Inside and out, animals were intent on taking over my space, crowding me out, and in the case of the bugs, crawling all over me. Yuk!

The first venue was a movie set version of the front hall of my childhood home in Wynnewood, Pennsylvania. Insects of myriad shapes and sizes started showing up and creeping around on the black and white square tile floor. As my brothers and I stood watchfully by, dozens of bugs crawled in under the door from the garden that separated our house from the one next door. At first, I wasn't particularly upset by the invasion.

Soon though, the advancing troops began morphing into large fluorescent green plastic facsimiles of themselves.

The odd-looking critters began climbing onto me, where they stuck leech-like to my bare arms and legs. As quickly as I could remove them, more would attach to my skin, many bigger than the giant scarab beetles that haunted our wicker laundry basket in my Egypt days.

While I was put off by the dream bugs, I was not as horrified as you'd think I should have been from the description. Not, that is, until a giant prehistoric-looking fellow on four legs made his way into the house through the now wide open door to the garden. But in a flash, he and the bugs were gone, and I found myself and my dream entourage standing on a grassy, pine-covered knoll.

Trond and I lived in **Egypt** the year Nora turned one, and our son Teg turned seven. It was a trial by fire (literally!), thanks to searing heat and few conveniences for this struggling young mother from the cool, comfy West. But, like the year I spent teaching in India right after college (more about that one soon), I wouldn't trade my experiences there for all the conveniences in the world.

❖ ❖ ❖

We watched as black panthers prowled the fields below us. The cats were big and muscular, their sleek black skins gleaming in the sunlight as they paced around not far from where we stood. Awed by their magnificence, it took a moment to realize they were dangerous and could quickly move in on us. I had better get moving if I didn't want to become someone's dinner. I scrambled up and out onto the limb of a nearby pine tree, safe in my perch before the dream ended.

In the last, most provocative dream, I stood with others at the edge of a deep mine-like pit. I watched as a great surge of water arose in a pool far below, engulfing and appearing to drown a small woman in a bathing suit. The scene unfolded so deep in the pit that it was hard for me to tell—and being a dream, hard to remember later—whether the woman had been lying on a beach by the water's edge or perhaps wading in what was shallow water before the mysterious flood.

Either way, she was a goner now. I stared intently from my distant perch as a black clad underwater rescue team approached to recover the tiny pale figure, curled lifelessly in the fetal position. I, on the other hand, felt oddly alive and self-connected as I watched the drama unfold from afar. I knew when I woke up that something powerful was afoot.

Rather than analyzing them, I trusted that beneath the surface, the dreams were doing with me what needed to be done, without knowing quite what that is—or needing to. And I have *no* idea how that subtle work of Rory's could have prompted such a night!

PART II

Home to My Indian Roots

October into November 2004

October into November 2004

Divine Delhi

I had been drawn to a return trip to this country where I once lived, and which I love, by an email from the Woodstock International School in Mussoorie, India. Quite improbably, the day after graduating from college in New York City, I'd headed for that school in the remote Himalayan foothills, to teach English and French to American and European missionary kids. Talk about culture shock (and I don't mean India; I mean the missionary school culture versus the wild Columbia University sixties scene I had just left behind).

Four decades later, the Woodstock School was celebrating its 150th anniversary with a festive weekend and selection of tours, one of which I dearly wanted to take. It was time to go back and, though Trond had never been especially drawn to India, he was cool with it all. After weeks of gearing up, the two of us arrived in India in the middle of the other night, bleary-eyed and expectant.

Like many tourists, we have begun our trip in Delhi. We've chosen to stay three nights at the Imperial Hotel, which, though under (loud!) construction, is still as elegant and delightful as it must have been in its English colonial heyday. The plan is to help our bodies catch up gently (and luxuriously) with the time-space leap we asked them to make, before setting off on our diverse and rigorous itinerary.

We were met at the Delhi airport by representatives of Uday Tours, a travel agency recommended by the school. Uday has also lined up guides for us from Delhi to Rajasthan. Our Delhi guide is a massive fellow with the same name as India's first Prime Minister, Jawaharlal Nehru. But as this Jawaharlal told us when I commented on his illustrious moniker, "Nehru was a big man and I am a small one." I laughed to myself as I mentally compared the late slight statesman in the trim Nehru jacket with the tall beefy man standing next to me. But I knew what he meant.

Jawaharlal and the scores of other guides we see here with tourists in tow seem profoundly bored. Guides earn their money on tips and commissions from sales they persuade us, their tourist clients, to make. No surprise then that we go to shops as often as they dare work them in between stops at genuine tourist sites. Jawaharlal is making out well, as we've surprised ourselves by spending oodles on Kashmiri rugs and shawls, Udaipur miniatures, jewelry and myriad equally beautiful if less consequential things. We've been buying like fiends, on the perfectly logical pretext of having special gifts to give back home. But come on people, once our newfound treasures make it through our front door, few are probably going to make it out again. Like much about this astounding country, Indian arts and crafts are beyond seductive.

Nearly everywhere we stop to shop, we are invited to sit, sip tea with biscuits, and be formally presented with fabulous goods. We are gracefully regaled about "exceptional values" by appealing merchants. Most fun is arriving at the cost, which we come to after haggling long and hard—and we hope, skillfully—enough so that in most cases everybody leaves smiling. More than one merchant was smiling a little too broadly, I thought. And I definitely heard tittering at the rug shop when we were not quite out of earshot. But given the gorgeous wares, who cares if we lose a round or two?

Yesterday, with Jawaharlal cheering us on, usually shop-phobic Trond and I bought no less than four used Kashmiri carpets, which I infinitely preferred to the sleek new ones. The merchant at first resisted my request to remove old rugs from the wall so I could take a better look. I soon realized why. The old rugs were there on commission, to be sold on behalf of destitute Kashmiris forced to put family treasures up for sale. Merchant and guide make more money on new ones.

But I prevailed. After I shook my head at every last (ugly) new rug he expectantly brought out, the frustrated shopkeeper finally gave in and lugged some old commissioned carpets from the back. I fell in love with their naturally dyed, jewel-like colors and intricate designs, each one more beautiful than the last. We must have spent two hours at that rug shop, the final one taken up with the requisite good-natured bargaining, which I thoroughly enjoyed and dare say am pretty good at, thanks to that long-ago year in Egypt, replete as it was with haggling.

Most entrancing for me so far was our trip through Old Delhi. It may be a dot on the map of India's sprawling capital, but it is the heart, rife with an astonishing mix of man and beast. Streets teem with hawkers, oxen, goats, bicycles, rickshaws, chickens, motorbikes heaped with entire families, and the ubiquitous teensy three-wheeled taxis. Saffron-robed sadhus, bearded priests and sundry holy men greeted us at the religious sanctuaries we visited in too-quick succession.

Men, who seem less productive than women in India, were drinking chai and chatting in the cramped three-walled stalls that often pass for stores. The Jain men with their protective mouth guards, worn to keep from killing any bugs that might fly into their mouths, mingled with the throngs of more ordinary looking shoppers. Only now and then did we spot brilliant sari-clad Hindu and black-garbed Muslim women moving quickly along, their covered heads down.

Beggars and cripples abound, in Old Delhi and everywhere we've been. But I am relieved to see far fewer lepers than I saw forty years ago. Most heart-wrenching this time was a single leper on all fours, like a dog, wearing two pairs of worn shoes, one on his hands, the other on his feet.

To step into Old Delhi is to enter a warm embrace. Relax and you melt into it, carried along—and practically away—by its ebb and flow, a stream of life as old as time. It appears chaotic and even crazy to our western mind-driven eyes. But at the level of heart, it seems just right to me, part of a higher organization that I only begin to intuit and am moved by. As we emerged from our air-conditioned car into the hot, filthy streets of Old Delhi, Jawaharlal in tow, I felt at once at home.

To step into Old Delhi is to enter a warm embrace. Relax and you melt into it, carried along — and practically away — by its ebb and flow, a stream of life as old as time.

I was uplifted as we eased our way through the not-so-madding crowds and into the temples and mosques that still serve as ritual containers for India's irrepressible spirit. I have felt more alive in India, more consistently *here now* than I have felt since…

well, probably since I was last in India, or sometimes ten to twenty years ago at the Kripalu Center, which being an ashram headed by an Indian guru, had a thing or two in common with this country I love and appreciate so much.

Of course, I am on vacation, and one that more than any other (even to China), has thrown me totally out of my element. So it's no surprise I would feel more present, aware and alive than I do at home. I have often felt alive like this in Mexico, and a few years ago, too, during a wonderful week in Venice—cultures older and gentler than ours. But I feel more present still in India, more of me asked to show up more often and pay more attention to whatever happens to be going down.

High in the Himalayas

An awful lot has been going down—and coming up— for me on this trip, especially since we got up into the Himalayas. They say you can't go home again. The truth is you can *only* go home again, so long as you understand that *the heart is where home is*, as well as the other way around. Climbing, as we just have, up from the great Indian plains and high into those mothers of all mountains, I went home again all right.

It was a beautiful fall day earlier this week

The truth is you can only go home again, so long as you understand that the heart is where home is, as well as the other way around.

45

when Trond and I and Gautam, the lovely 19-year-old son of our tour guides Tenzing and Tsering, set off by car on a five-day trip to the mouth of the fabled Ganges. Just a few kilometers out the Tehri Road from the spartan Mussoorie hotel where we and our fellow travelers had gathered to adjust to the altitude and prepare for the trip, we rounded a long slow bend. The stunning snow-covered Himalayan peaks, which had eluded us entirely in Mussoorie, suddenly shot into view, piercing my heart like a spray of white arrows.

The stunning snow-covered Himalayan peaks suddenly shot into view, piercing my heart like a spray of white arrows.

How can I tell you, how do I put into plain black letters on a blank page, the breathtaking sense of my whole self coming intensely alive that I felt when I got my first short glimpse of Himalayan heaven? For the next many hours, till well after dark, we drove—or were driven, thank God!—part of a caravan of five vehicles, snaking back and up into these greatest of all mountains. The farther we went, the more of them were revealed to us. It was a day like no other.

As we wound our circuitous way up, up, then down again, and around the steep, narrow, bumpy mountain road, hour after hour, on and on toward Gangotri near the Ganges' mouth, each hairpin turn opened up another spectacular vista. It was beauty so grand it threw me right out of my ordinary mind and into Mother Mountain's arms. I might as well have been on drugs.

Thank God for that. For if I'd been stuck in my drunken monkey mind, as yogis call our ordinary ego-driven mental state, I'd have been scared shitless. We should not have survived that drive! Many don't, which might be reason to walk it, as the intrepid author Stephen Alter did.

Yet we did survive, of course, braving a long day of steep, sharp bends. We were counting heavily on our skillful driver's capacity to honk, our sole defense against whatever car, overloaded truck or bus might be heading straight for us around the next curve. For did I mention there was almost always only one lane, and that we were often mere feet from the precipitous mountain's edge, looking down, when we dared, at sheer rock wall drops of a few thousand feet or more?

During much of the drive we followed the path of the legendary Ganges (which Indians call Ganga), India's most holy of rivers. Its water is thought so pure and sacred that a few of its drops must pass through the lips of all good Hindus on their way from this life to the next. No wonder!

Its gorgeous ice blue waters kept us constant, riveting company. Sometimes we were down by the roaring river's edge. At others, we were up on the ledge of a sharply towering cliff gaping through dusty windows at what—after another long, steep switchback climb—became a silver thread far below us. Almost always Ganga was visible, inexorably guiding us toward her mouth.

The mighty Ganga, the massive towering Himalayas. We were on the long-anticipated *Yatra* trip: a pilgrimage to the source of the sacred Ganges, itself the source of much of India's great Hindu mythology, and so, of my own spiritual heritage through yoga. We had not been given a precise schedule of our several-day tour from Mussoorie and back again (a sixteen-hour roundtrip drive, as it turned out). But our stopping point for the first few nights was Gangotri, which translates as "mouth of the Ganges."

It's where Ganga used to begin, before the glacier receded to Gaumukh.

Gangotri is an established spiritual—and now also commercial and residential—community embanked on both sides of the rushing Ganga, with the snowcapped Himalayan peaks uprising close to the river's banks. I fell head over heels for the place, even stricken and restricted as I felt by its cold, sharp, and to my lungs (if not Trond's), dangerously thin air. At 10,300 feet, Gangotri is as high as I've been on this earth and it nearly knocked my thick wool socks off.

Though it is still October, if barely, the weather at night up there was literally freezing. Fortunately after much debate (Trond always opting to pack less), I had bought and brought warm jackets, hats, scarves, mittens, shawls, long undies and thermal layers sufficient to clothe a small country. Not so fortunately, the place we called home for what became three nights in Gangotri, was a cluster of tiny spartan rooms containing no heat source whatsoever. The rooms were piled on top of each other around a central *open-air* courtyard, which became our living and dining space—rain, shine or snow showers (and we experienced them all).

Here sat our sole source of warmth, a small tin can fire, encircled by a bunch of old white plastic chairs. We—the supposed guests at this (summer) "guest house"—and our band of bedraggled ever cheerful Nepalese coolies all huddled around that little fire and fed it thin sticks with a shared sense of responsibility and entitlement. A motley crew we were too, we guests swathed beyond recognition in our layers of warming Western gear and the small coolies clad only in light jackets or sweaters, with often nothing on their feet but flip-flops even up on the rocky trail.

Our roofless Gangotri quarters sat one story up at Ganga's edge. Every meal and conversation—every moment—was accompanied by the thundering river below, still swollen with the after-effects of recent monsoon rains. For three hours each night, the river's roar was accompanied by the less sonorous, near-deafening mechanical hum of a generator across the river, which provided electricity for us and the rest of Gangotri. Then it was lights out, when most of us headed for bed and the prospect of remaining every bit as cold as we'd been outside, even under the covers.

These consisted of large, grubby oblong bags like the sacks donkeys carry on their backs here. They were filled with heavy rough material that might have been straw— and/or, dear God, dung. While none too cozy to start with, this awkward getup also made it impossible to turn over, a situation exacerbated by our own awkward getups— bundled as we were in every bit of warm clothing we'd brought.

But the sleeping arrangements were as nothing compared with midnight trips to the dank, pitch dark excuse for a bathroom. It was lit only by a candle in a coke bottle, until it burned out around midnight, as I quickly learned to my dismay. The toilets didn't flush, though there was plenty of cold running water—all over the icy cement floor. Still, just as with camping trips years ago, I wonder now how much the extreme physical hardship I experienced in Gangotri contributed to the quiet exuberance I felt the entire time we were there.

It was a joy to emerge from our frigid cubicle each morning into the still-chilly sunlit blue and be handed a steaming cup of café au lait Indian style. Better still was the ubiquitous spicy chai masala, which I've come to love so much I plan to make it for myself at home. We'd stamp our feet, rub our mittened hands together and watch our clouds of breath rise to meet each other in the crisp thin air. If the coolies, who got up earlier than we did, hadn't already occupied them all, we'd pull a plastic chair close to the fire and all but thrust our hands into it.

Other mornings when I felt warm enough to eschew the fire for a while, I'd stand at our common balcony's edge, gazing straight up, awestruck by the sharp white peaks looming above me. Looking down, I'd see the odd intrepid autumn pilgrim (always male) taking a near-naked ritual morning plunge in the frosty, rapidly flowing river, a stone's throw from where I stood. More modest sari-and-overcoat-clad women stooped carefully at river's edge to collect the holy water in jugs—for themselves, and as gifts for loved ones down on the plains. Lazy pilgrims could purchase tiny glass bottles of "Ganga water" at any of dozens of souvenir stalls in town.

On the Way to Gaumukh

After a few days adjusting to the thin air of Gangotri, our big day of trekking toward Ganga's source in Gaumukh arrived. Our intrepid band of Yatra travelers set off a little later than planned on mule back, most of us riding, and when that was too dangerous, all of us walking on our own steam. By the time we stopped for lunch, we'd gone nine rocky kilometers and climbed another 2,000 feet from the more than 10,000 we'd been getting used to in Gangotri. We were most of the way to where we were to spend the night in tents, before another day of trekking the last several hours to the glacier that is Ganga's mouth.

But getting to Gaumukh was not to be. It was two o'clock when we arrived at the chai stall, a gaggle of tents and carpets where we dismounted for food and drink. We'd been on the narrow, slippery, sometimes steep and always unnervingly high mountain trail since 9:30 in the morning. As we picked at our meager unsavory meal, heavy gray clouds overtook what all morning had been a bright blue sky. The temperature had already dropped precipitously, and most of our none-too-young crew of fifteen were hungry, cold and tired.

By the time snow began to fall, I for one had had enough drama and daring-do by mule back, the trail sometimes so constricted we had to dismount and cling to near-sheer rock walls in order to pass and avoid falling to certain death. So while I had loved almost every minute of it so far, by lunch time it hit me that, sooner or later, we would have to repeat this trip, and much more, in reverse. I was opting for sooner—and began whispering to Trond and others about possibly not going on.

Snow could make the five-kilometer trail to our tent site cold, slippery and even more dangerous. And there was the chance we would get snowed in en route and not reach the glacial waterfall at all. It also occurred to me we might be so delayed we wouldn't make it back to Mussoorie in time for the anniversary celebration, the main reason I'd decided to return to India in the first place. I didn't for anything want to risk missing the chance to reconnect with the people, places and feelings that had opened my heart and radically touched my life those forty years ago.

So over lunch with Trond's help, I planted seeds of an early return to Gangotri in the ear of our intrepid leader Tenzing. As the snow kept coming, and we travelers huddled together in the chai tent awaiting the verdict, Tenzing and his aides consulted about our future.

It was a group of damned good sports, of all ages and fitness levels, we were traveling with. Though it later became clear I was far from alone, few of us fessed up at the time that we wanted to turn around. A few were eager to press on. So maybe if I'd kept my mouth shut, we would have made it to Gaumukh and been the better for it. We'll never know, because my fears, fueled by too many stories of Everest climbers biting the dust (*snow dust*, that is), got the better of me, along with my overstrained body. For better or worse, I selfishly used my influence to affect us all.

For better or worse, I selfishly used my influence to affect us all.

Several uncertain minutes passed. The snow fell steadily as we women scrambled to find discrete places to pee. It was always an interesting issue on this trip, the makeshift outdoor "bathroom" stops (often with no more than a held-up cloth to crouch behind). The order came down: "Mount your mules. I want everybody on a mule this time," Tenzing said. "We're heading back to Gangotri." Even Trond, who to everyone's amazement had been walking beside the mule guides every step of the way up—like the ox he insists he is—climbed on a mule for the trip back.

After several hours of picking our way oh, so carefully down the trail through falling snow, we finally arrived at dusk at our guest house by the Ganges. Proving once more how everything is relative, that frigid, ramshackle place of ours suddenly looked better than good—almost like home sweet home. And once Joshi began his evensong for us, there was no doubt about it—we were home again, where the heart is.

Joshi on Fire

Evenings, spent riverside around our little fire, were the most joyous times in Gangotri. No doubt the bootlegged alcohol lifted our spirits and loosened our tongues. For in blatant violation of holy Gangotri's ban on booze, meat and eggs, our guides dispensed liquor freely from their cubicle-cum-bar, along with feeding us eggs for breakfast. God knows what the coolies were on, but it smelled a lot like pot. After dinner, the bravest among our Yatra band would gather in the chill darkness to drink, chat and sometimes to sing, the Nepalese men sitting or crouching among us.

The evening we returned from our unsuccessful trek was the most magical of all. The adorable Gautam, who had become our friend on our shared death-defying car ride to Gangotri, brought out his guitar and began to strum and sing, familiar English melodies mixed in with Hindi tunes and a few songs he had written himself. We were all having a marvelous time. Then, during a lull in the music making, something wonderful and unexpected happened. Above the conversation and roar of the river, came a high haunting wail.

It took a moment to realize it was Joshi, the smallest and most engaging of our mild-mannered coolies. Leaning back in his chair, eyes closed, mouth wide open—as if in a trance all his own—he was singing what we later learned was a traditional Nepalese folk song. More than singing, he was pouring his heart out for us, for himself—and for God, it seemed. As he continued, Gautam began carefully to pick out the tune on his guitar. Now with full accompaniment, Joshi leapt out of his chair like a man possessed and, still singing, began dancing wildly around us and the fire.

Now with full accompaniment, Joshi leapt out of his chair like a man possessed and, still singing, began dancing wildly around us and the fire.

Faster and faster he twirled—dervish-like—sometimes straight up with arms and legs fully outstretched, sometimes crouching while still managing to spin. He sang strongly and sweetly all the while, as the rest of us watched, mesmerized by the fierce joy that inspired him. Joshi was on fire, and for many magical moments there beneath the starlit Himalayas at the Ganges' edge, he lit *us* up too. He ignited our hearts with the fire of his passion—which given the sacredness of where we sat, may well have been his own very particular expression of divine love!

Tears at Dahlia Bank

Though I have felt cold and out of breath up here in the Himalayas where the air is rare, my chest has filled with spirit till I've felt it might just burst. Even more than in the rest of India, I am uncommonly alive, sometimes poignantly, sometimes joyously aware of *being exactly how and where I am*, and nowhere else. I have entered the terrain of Eckhart Tolle's potent *now*. I am here, with little sense of the future—though at times in Mussoorie, where we've returned after the Yatra trip and where I lived and worked those forty years ago, with more than a little sense of the past.

As we arrived at Woodstock's 150th Anniversary Celebration on Friday, a tour of old Mussoorie houses was underway. Built by the mission churches, each given a romantic British name, these homes had offered generations of colonial English, and later American missionaries and other foreigners, summer respite from the steamy plains where they worked. Dozens of such once lovely properties dot the steep, heavily wooded hillside above and below the spread-out school buildings.

There was one house in particular I was dying to see, on the highly unlikely chance it might be among the few on the tour. With barely an hour left before the hillside open houses would be closed to visitors—and with the makeshift tour booth about to shut down—I just managed to get my hands on a list of the names. Whipping through them, I was astonished to find the only one I cared about halfway down the page: *Dahlia Bank!* My heart leapt. Yes, you can go home again.

Earlier in the nineteenth century when the English still ruled India, Dahlia Bank was a boarding house run by the Indian grandparents of an Anglo-Indian cellist named Tristan. Like me, Tristan was twenty-one years old when I arrived in India in 1964. The English were long gone and Tristan's grandparents both dead. He lived on the isolated

Dahlia Bank compound alone, except for his two dogs and a Brahmin cook with his little grand boy. Tristan and I met and fell in love. I spent every spare moment that year at Dahlia Bank, and I left part of my heart there when my Woodstock School teaching stint was done. I'd have given anything to see that old house again.

I spent every spare moment that year at Dahlia Bank, and I left part of my heart there when my Woodstock School teaching stint was done.

But could Trond and I possibly make it up the steep rugged hillside in time to get in on the tour? Could I find it forty years later? What would the place where I spent a year—in love, at the edge of the world and very near the top of it—look like now? How would it be for me to see it again?

It was no easy feat arranging for a taxi to take us from the school up the 2,000 precipitous, circuitous feet, and out to what I remembered as the last house on the ridge by Sister's Bazaar. We waited in the taxi line at the school and took what we could get when our turn came. Our driver spoke almost no English and drove a wreck of a car. He had no idea where Dahlia Bank was and was not remotely interested in finding out. I was less than optimistic as we set out.

Because I was persistent, or just because the driver was being paid well, we eventually managed to make our way up and out in the general direction where I thought I recalled Tristan's house was. After several false starts, dead ends, backups, and queries that I insisted our driver make of the odd passerby, we arrived minutes before the tour witching hour at a narrow, dangerously rocky lane (if you could call it that). But wouldn't you know, the way to Dahlia Bank was under heavy construction and the workers indicated (accurately as it turned out) it was all but impassable. Though the driver had no intention of proceeding, I insisted, obsessed as I had become with reaching the house in time.

Slowly, bumpily—miraculously—the road crew gawking and squawking at the crazy people (and our driver almost apoplectic), we passed along the impassable way, landing up at last by a high rusted iron gate. Through it, I could make out the still whitewashed, now shabby green-shuttered bungalow I had called my second home away from home four decades ago. Dahlia Bank! Would anyone be there? How were we going to get past the gate, which looked to be firmly locked?

Trond and I piled out of the tiny taxi and asked our by now extremely disgruntled driver to wait. As we approached the tall fence, one of the ubiquitous Indian mutts appeared out of nowhere yapping at us from the other side. Soon followed a pleasant-looking Indian man who spoke little English, while we, of course, knew no Hindi to *speak* of. But understanding we wanted to come into the yard, he thoughtfully unlocked the gate for us. He communicated with shrugged shoulders and a look of regret that the owners were not home and the house was locked. *Damn.*

We gathered the man was one of the caretakers who live in small huts located on these former mission properties. The huts used to house servants, like Tristan's cook at Dahlia Bank. Now, though, we learned they were reserved for people hired to protect permanent tenants' possessions when they are not home (never an issue in my day). The caretaker let us wander around Tristan's yard, and I peered eagerly through the small windows lining the concrete porch, where Tristan and I used to sit for hours on end with his prized black labs, Dusky and Beauty.

Tristan and I were often joined on weekends at Dahlia Bank by a potpourri of our favorite Woodstock School students: my still friend Cecilia, there for just a year; John Alter, the '60s beat poet among us, whose whole family had gone to Woodstock; his current girlfriend, a French Canadian hottie named Clare; a mature German intellectual, Helke, and a small dear Dutch boy named Bim—strangely wise for his eleven years—with whom Tristan liked to talk and play chess.

I thought as I sat to write this morning that I would have to wait till I got home and refer to a yellowed annotated black and white photo of us all, taken on Tristan's porch—if I could find my India box in the attic. But the names and faces of those special kids who shared my Himalayan experience bubbled right up from my heart, fresh as memories of my recent visit to Dahlia Bank.

Standing there the other day, I found myself gazing through thick evergreens, grown tall and mighty in the decades since I last saw them. Now, they nearly obscure the once splendid views of further Himalayan peaks and valleys I'd assumed would always be there. Though I didn't want to leave, our driver was waiting and there was no reason to stick around—until a car pulled up at the gate.

Yay! It was the young American family who lived there, returning as it turned out from guiding a Woodstock-related side trip into the mountains, like the one we had just returned from. Their business, and why they lived here in Mussoorie, they told us, was to lead a variety of treks in the

Himalayas. Warm and welcoming, they invited us inside, exhausted though they must have been.

I was thrilled at first. But as I made my curious way from one spare, gloomy room to another, I felt less emotion than I'd expected to. Tristan was long gone to a new life (with a wife) in Australia, and the inside of the house, though hardly updated, felt oddly unfamiliar to me. Then I wandered into a side room by myself and—boom—the past erupted. This, I realized, was the room where Tristan and I slept on the many nights when I had snuck out of the (strict) missionary-peopled dorm where I lived and made my way alone through the darkness up the slippery slopes to see him.

In that bedroom forty years later, I burst into tears (and do again now as I write these words). Retreating to the spartan bathroom adjoining the bedroom, I struggled to collect myself. I badly wanted to be able to break down and let my heart break over what had been and gone those forty years ago. Instead, I put the brakes on, for Trond's sake and out of pride, in front of strangers. After a couple of minutes, I emerged from my long-ago lovers' chamber as dry-eyed as possible.

We talked with the couple living there, who were curious to learn about the history of their house, before taking our leave. But just as we were about to get into the taxi, I stopped. "I need to go back," I told Trond. So I did, to the rampant chagrin of our poor driver. Ignoring his yells, I walked quickly past the house to the edge of the cliff on which the property sits and dissolved again into the tears I had stifled inside. I wept like the baby I'd been forty years ago. I cried my heart out, alone, and then in Trond's arms, when he most kindly came to find and comfort me.

God knows what I was—and am now—weeping for, but I can guess. I cry for the forty years come and gone, for the impending inevitability of my death, and for the love of Tristan, whom I am unlikely ever to see again. I cry for the bittersweet joy we knew (knowing deep down it would only last a year) in that magical Dahlia Bank at the further reaches of the Himalayan foothills. I cry because I am almost old. Despite the wet tears running down my cheeks, the juice in me is drying up—I will soon be as devoid of the life I once contained as Dahlia Bank now feels to me to be.

But I cry most, I know, for the loss of unbridled passion, innocence, and what must have been the greatest, most unconditional love and devotion ever showered upon me. Tristan adored me like no one ever had since my doting grandmother Molly, who died when I was nine, and I've got his letters somewhere in the attic to prove it. His love was that of an angel for an angel.

The slim beautiful Anglo-Indian orphan worshipped and lifted me up that year from the often-grim world of the missionaries I lived and taught with. He was an angel to me. And I must have seemed like an angel to him too, showing up out of the blue as I did—beautiful, warm, sexy, and eager to add my light and love to what had been his tough life, and in a very different way, my own.

Tristan was the illegitimate son of an English sea captain and his Indian lover. He had been scraping out a living teaching music following the death of the grandparents who had raised him. A classical musician in a part of the world with little use for that, he was a not-quite-Indian who had never left India. But I left India, leaving him behind to fend for himself again. Do my steady tears also speak of guilt for my heartless abandonment of the one person who held me precious as life itself? I am sorry, dear Tristan, and I'd like to find a way to let you know that.

Back on the Farm

Today is Mom's eighty-eighth birthday, and while she—usually the more inveterate and intrepid traveler among us—has long been staying put, I've been to ancient India and back for the second time in my life. I'm glad I decided to write today, since noting the date may help this disoriented daughter remember to wish her Mom a happy birthday. But I can't call yet. It is 4:30 a.m. in Pennsylvania, the day after Trond and I returned from our trip of a lifetime.

We left Delhi in the wee hours yesterday morning and arrived, via Milan to Washington Dulles in mid-afternoon of the same yesterday, thirty hours of travel time later. Phew! What may have been the longest day of my life is now exacerbated by a ten-and-a-half hour time difference, leaving my body in a puddle, and my mind a muddle of wild impressions.

The Woodstock Anniversary Weekend was almost as wonderful as the rest of the trip. But just as with Tristan's house, the spread-out hillside school buildings we got to tour on Saturday felt none too familiar. I suppose that was partly because, unlike Tristan's, they'd been completely revamped. Thanks to a drastic renovation of the girl's dorm, I couldn't even find the little whitewashed rooms where I'd lived across the hall from a pair of missionary twins—with no hot water, bats in the bedroom, scorpions in the bath, and monkeys chattering and clattering on the metal roof.

Though parts of the monsoon-orchid-strewn paths I had taken up to Tristan's had been enhanced with steps and ramps, the way was still so long, roundabout and steep that Trond couldn't believe I used to climb it daily (and no wonder I look rail thin in the few photos from that intense year!). But except for the distant white peaks, little of Mussoorie and Woodstock was as I remembered, often rendering both my memories and this new experience surreal. Had I really been there? Was *I* the same person I'd been then? Yes, and yes and no. That year felt like lifetimes ago.

For the 150th anniversary feast—held out under a bright night sky—we dressed up and dressed warmly, the foothill weather having turned unseasonably cool. I was delighted when Tom Alter asked to sit next to me at dinner. *Tommy* was the youngest of the two Alter brothers I taught, once a tow-headed ninth-grade French student, now a handsome, graying, bearded Bollywood actor. He's an Indian citizen, fluent in Hindi, and something of a hero at Woodstock and elsewhere.

The nostalgia (and the reality check) of seeing Tom, and my other students who had come back, transformed into late middle-aged adults was almost unbearable (even if Tom said I didn't look a day older than they did). I rocketed between the aging woman I am and the girl I'd been. I cried when I needed to and smiled broadly the rest of the time, at the sheer joy of what once was—or what remained to be remembered anyway, of a mind-blowing twelve months four decades ago.

It is too soon to know how my much-anticipated return to the country that blew my heart open long ago may affect me—heart, soul and every other way—this time around. My first trip, with Tristan in the Himalayas and in Hyderabad—and traveling the country in third-class trains with Cecilia, two young lone Western women finding our way in a sea of South Indians—set the stage for my fall into yoga and a lineage of gurus. It irrevocably colored who I am. This trip, to the Himalayas, Delhi and Rajasthan (which I'm not moved to write about, but which I savored to the hilt), also made deep impressions whose impact on me, however, very much remains to be seen.

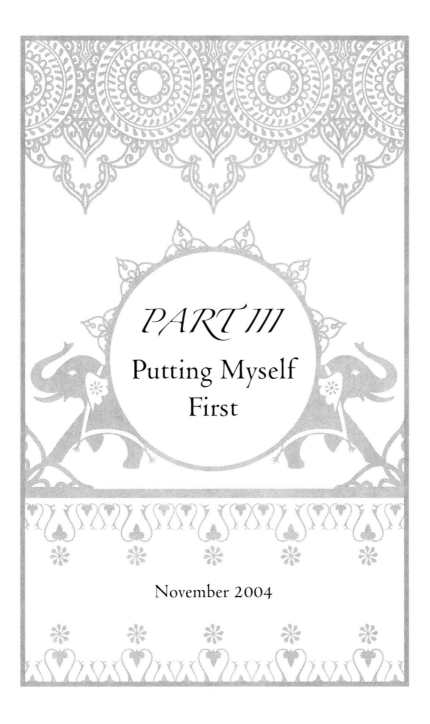

PART III
Putting Myself First

November 2004

November 20, 2004

Leaving No Trace

This morning I allowed my dear self to become confused and lost again. That usually means I am overdue for journaling my way to clarity. It's a dreary Saturday. Trond has been called out to our landfill gas recovery plant in Lebanon for a repair job, bless his heart. I have nothing more compelling calling me (if you can call it *calling*) than errands, which except for picking up a good loaf of bread at the Farmer's Market could easily go undone.

What *is* calling me, when I stop long enough to pay attention, is *how very much my body hurts*. My discomfort may be less today than it has been recently, thanks to my having committed much of yesterday to taking good care of myself. But most days lately, I am in near agony, my stiff, sore neck only the most chronic manifestation that something is very wrong with me. That's not just in my head, where we know a wounded Inner Child still lives and breathes down that stiff neck of mine. No, nearly everywhere I look in my body I find physical pain as sharp as it is constant.

As I told Kimberly during a wonderfully uplifting call yesterday, I am a whiz at going through the motions of "extreme self-care." That's what Ilana Rubenfeld called the rigorous attention to ourselves that she insisted on for her Synergists. Without putting too self-deprecating a spin on it, though, my efforts are a paltry sham next to what may be

Ilana Rubenfeld is the founder of the eponymous work in which I became certified as part of my journey to help myself and others break through fear to Source love. A pioneer in body-mind therapy (though she eschewed the "T" word), Ilana worked with Moshe Feldenkrais, Gestalt therapist Fritz Perls and other renowned teachers, on the way to creating her Rubenfeld Synergy Method. She holds high standards for practitioners of her work, notably in the realm of self-care.

❧ ❧ ❧

required to dissolve this pain of mine.

Yesterday, I spoke so eloquently to Kimberly that I wish I'd taped our call. But it may serve me to have to call forth again today what I knew so well then—who I am, and what I do and don't want to do about it. Suddenly I am struggling even to write. I feel myself being pulled back inside, where I spent much of yesterday in a rare and welcome peace. So I am pausing for a minute now to collect myself, wanting to wait and let my words emerge from that ground of being inside, which until now seemed as elusive today as it was alive and kicking yesterday.

What I so recently knew, as well as my name, is this: *It is time for a radical shift of my whole self toward God. Toward God* is not what I said to Kimberly. It comes to me now, though, from somewhere that is both me and more than me. I must shift toward God, who lives in the bones and muscles—the juicy, fertile ground of me. Not in the mind but in the marrow is where God lives. *To know myself as God I must stop the fucking mind games and come home to this body that hurts.*

I am That. I know it, and I do not have to lead programs at Kripalu or write books to prove it, as my ego-mind thinks. But only—*only*—when I stop and sit in the NOW, the here and the nowhere else, like this, do I consistently get to remember that I am God and that it—all that I might want to *achieve* in this short lifetime—is already being done through me. I don't have to lift a frigging finger, and what's more, to be of real service, I *must* not, unless and until I want to.

I say to anyone who is interested, "Do only what you

> **"I am That"** is the shortened version of "I am that I am," a famous Old Testament phrase with many interpretations. It comes to me often as I write and seems to be my way of acknowledging that I am perfect as I am, and part of the perfect indivisible whole of life.
>
> ❧ ❧ ❧

love." It sounds absurdly simple. But I am coming to see what a profound statement it is, a "divine order" almost. It has been given to me, yes, to share, as I've been doing sometimes cavalierly, often sincerely, here. But more than ever, "Do only what you love" is an order *given for me to practice*, an edict about a new way to live.

Thy will be done, Oh Lord, not mine. There's another of those radical divine edicts I like to toss around. Out it popped. I am laughing aloud at the paradox, the apparent contradiction between my two English mantras: "Do only what you love" and "Thy will be done, Oh Lord, not mine."

But really, what I *love*—what truly pleases me most—*is* to do God's will alone, not my often ill-informed, ill-conceived one. I am never more happy or fulfilled (let alone less alone) than when I leave ego-mind at the door, sink into my tender heart, and give myself over entirely to what is—God's will, if you will. Then only am I *That*: one—and at one—with the reality I call God.

To do only what we love, and to love what we do, we must learn to discern divine will and align our whole self with it. It is easy for me to *say* that, even with great conviction. What can seem harder is to cut through the thicket of clinging old habits, which keep me doing what I've always done, pushing and pulling myself this way and that in hopes others will love me, and I will be better able to love myself (let alone love myself *as God*).

I have been working for years with a client who is caught in the self-annihilating habit of doing whatever she thinks it takes to keep people happy with her, so they will love her—especially men who aren't good for her. Her behavior has seemed to me, and to her, extreme. It has driven her to exhaustion, depression, even to near starvation—the brink. My case is more subtle. Or is it?

The development of a now nearly immobile head and neck, lately riddled with sharp shooting pains, suggests a case can be made that my case is not as subtle as I like to think. It hardly matters who is worse off, my client or I. As I accuse her of doing, I too have betrayed myself by not attending to God's will, at the deepest level of my being. I meet my basic needs all right. But I have ignored my holiest wants, the quiet and not-so-quiet promptings of a weary body and soul.

I meet my basic needs all right. But I have ignored my holiest wants, the quiet and not-so-quiet promptings of a weary body and soul.

My self-betrayal and the ways to correct it are subtle in this way: Unlike my client, I may not have to change much externally; as I often say, I go through many right motions. I sign up and show up regularly for exercise, massage and coaching; I sit in silence and write like this. I appear to nourish my body, mind and spirit, too, in ways that would do my once-teacher Ilana proud.

What needs to change—I say it again, but with more understanding and conviction—is only that *I become fully present with and for myself while I do those things that I do.*

It is time to return with renewed vigor to the radical self-respect and trust I began tapping into when I started working with Maha in August. I created and sustained a similar state of being yesterday doing next to nothing at home, then having next to nothing done to me on Rory's chiropractic table. Suddenly last summer, and again yesterday, I slipped past monkey mind and came to a sense of fullness—enoughness—that when I let it, infuses my belly, legs, guts and heart.

In that state of presence or *being,* I am relaxed, alert, and full of myself, of God—the Self of All. I am so fulfilled there is nothing to be done but bask. Although I *do* do stuff, the false sense of urgency and the furious passage of time all but disappear. The need to make a mark is replaced by the desire, if you can call it that, to leave no trace. Rather than wanting to be somebody and get attention, the call is to be nobody at all, and to pay attention, to the no-self of spirit manifest in me and everything else. I am as impersonal as a drop of rain, as eternal as the sunshine.

In this place of almost utter stillness, love enters to fill the cracks and crevasses, to make whole what has been lost and broken. When I come to rest supreme in the endless moment, my broken heart feels almost of a piece, and at peace, again. There is hope, too, for me to heal my aching body, by inhabiting and listening to it, and by living from its gentle primal wisdom, rather than from the dictates of rapacious mind inside a head that hurts and isn't happy about it.

I must finally take the risk—and it is a risk only from
ego's point of view—of offending the world to attend to
myself. I must be willing to be
seen as eccentric and selfish, a
wild, crazy fool who, if I were to
stop trying to please and impress
others once and for all, I might
just turn out to be—and be
glad and maybe better for it. In

*I must finally take
the risk of offending
the world to attend
to myself.*

the end, I might be (or be seen as) nothing of the sort. But
I'd best be willing to be real and rash enough to risk being
trashed, or I will be selling myself short.

Maha reminded me the other day how I have been
hiding out in my family again. She said I've been using
Trond and my householder duties to escape the rigors of
being authentic and true to myself—as I know how to be by
now. Instead of busying myself about the home and out in
larger world, it would be better to make time to stop and ask
sincerely, as God's instrument in the world, "What do I want
to do right now?" And *now*, and now again, *what is and isn't
mine to do?*

May I let God show me the way, by way of letting life
unfold through and around me from moment to moment—
as I pay attention to what calls me. I exhort my clients to
know and trust themselves. *You know who you are and what
you want*, I tell them. *Act from that place.* If I am to take this
spiritual scribe that I am further out into the world, I must
align my own behavior, day by day, minute by minute even,
with what I know on a good day to be true of, to and for *me*.
I must.

If, as Maha has said, I have an angel on each shoulder,
may I know their blessings in a life more truly and

peacefully lived. May I know and do my work as Thy will, trusting that where I am is where I am meant to be, and that you will show me what's next. Even as I get up soon to go forth into this day, guide me back again and again to myself, to my body and its unerring truth, a *truth* that passes all understanding. How lightly can I tread today, how little trace can I leave?

How lightly can I tread today, how little trace can I leave?

November 22, 2004

Weird and Wonderful Us

To act with authenticity, I must be willing not to act at all. Otherwise, whatever I do will have an edge of compulsion, which, however subtle, feeds the fear I am not enough. Ironically, that's the same fear that has had me *hiding out in my family,* as Maha keeps accusing me of doing. It's the bugaboo I looked into last time I wrote, about stepping outside my comfort zone and being willing to be seen as The Fool or Weirdo. If I were not afraid of stepping out of line and being judged—caught with my pants down, as I shamefully was once or twice in childhood—what would I do?

The answer comes almost too quickly. *I'd publish these journals and reveal myself and my odyssey to everyone I might be able to serve.* But wait a minute. That is not what spiritual authors do, talk about themselves like this. Who am I anyway, weak and stumbling as I can be, to offer myself with such terrifyingly detailed intimacy to those in search of the light? Why me?

In truth, I may be a scribe of rare and useful gifts precisely *because* I'm aware of and honest about my human doubts, fears and (I hope) weaknesses, along with my strengths. One day I know who I am, the next

In truth, I may be a scribe of rare and useful gifts precisely because I'm aware of and honest about my human doubts, fears and (I hope) weaknesses, along with my strengths.

I seem to have forgotten again, not the usual exemplar. But might I serve others best by presenting my foibles as well as my gifts of gab and a great heart? Mightn't I be able to help people get comfortable with their own strange mix of doubt and courage, weird and wonderful?

Many teachers I know, or know of, seem to have it all together—themselves, their lives, their stories of enlightenment. It looks neat and clean for them from over here. These men and women share their spiritual knowledge, or wisdom, as a *fait accompli*, as if they are complete in it and have passed over to the other side. They write and speak as if they aren't quite in physical bodies, and life isn't the holy hellish struggle for them that it is for us. Maybe for them it isn't; how would I know?

But for me, and I suspect you too, Bapuji's sober assessment that *all life is struggle*, the title of my favorite among all his talks, seems spot-on, and even if I feel more than a little anxious and uncertain about it all today, I may just be onto something.

November 23, 2004

Mysterious Joy

Who knows why, but yesterday I could not—or, okay, *would* not—rid myself of a gnawing anxiety that lasted all day. Vasudev, a great Kripalu teacher of mine, used to remind us that, when we say we cannot do something, we almost always mean we don't *want* to do it and just don't want to admit it, even to ourselves. Vasudev was right about that.

So yesterday apparently I did not want peace. I wanted to fret that I'm wasting my life and fooling myself to think that I'm getting free. Must be a game I still like to play. Yesterday's anxiety, which felt like an actual weight around my neck and fist in my chest, is for the most part gone. My personal version of Bapuji's "all life is struggle" scenario has abated and I can breathe again.

As I inhale, I feel the antithesis of anxious. A quiet joy tugs at me from within, inviting me to close my eyes and relax into it. So I do, as I sit alone here again this morning—except for the cat on my lap—until Cynthia arrives soon to clean the house. Trond left early to go tend our Lebanon plant again today, freeing our plant manager, Bob, to go off on his sure-to-be-futile annual bear hunt. As Trond says about it every year, thank God he never even sees one!

I made a fire this morning, and its gentle crackling breaks what would be dead silence but for the soft sound of the heater. Every now and then its mechanical hum pulses up through the wide wooden floorboards separating our second floor living room from the kitchen down in the bowels of this old house, soon to have a birthday of its own—200 in 2012. About as old as I felt yesterday.

Why today am I bright and cheerful, making a world of difference from yesterday? It's as if I am *in* a different world. Am I better rested? Nothing else I can think of changed. I still hurt, and l have no more idea than before how to use what Maha assures me are my prodigious gifts—as seeker, teacher, writer and coach. But today my future fate doesn't matter so much.

It seems enough to have sat here for the last hour writing, and then to have stopped writing (while I straightened the house so Cynthia can clean), and now to be writing again. Writing, tidying, scurrying about or sitting still—it is just the same to me this morning. *I* am the same calm, composed Suzanne all the while. Go figure.

Though I am in more physical pain today than yesterday, the *I* that is not my body knows she is okay. And knowing I am more than this failing body must be enough to sustain me. Today I trust that life is a mystery and that I've been doing a half decent job of making the most of it—by slowing down, learning to be with the unknown and with myself as an instrument of divine play.

I may yet be called to greater service in the world, as Maha implies I should and will be. But when I am with myself fully and truly, the burning need to act abates. The familiar urge to *do* something to make an impression, on myself and others, is absorbed by the spaciousness of my being. It feels fine to sit here taking myself in, instead of making something of myself for the good of others.

When I am with myself fully and truly, the burning need to act abates.

And isn't it good—for everybody—for me to feel as relatively contented as I do today? Isn't it better to do little and be happy with myself, than to get stuff done as I did yesterday while feeling discontented? But will it as I might, contentment comes and goes with a will of its own, perversely oblivious to my perfectly reasonable desire to hold onto it for all it is worth.

God knows I tried to accept yesterday's discontent—acceptance being the closest thing I know to a magic bullet to dispel unwelcome moods. To accept or *welcome* the unwelcome is by definition to change that dynamic, isn't it? At the same time, I can't help thinking that if I were *doing* more I wouldn't have the time or inclination to fret so much that I am not doing enough, *am* not enough.

There's an old adage that says something about how keeping busy helps us forget our troubles, and isn't that the American Way? But my approach has been nearly the opposite. Sit with your troubles, I say; do nothing and wait. Let ill feelings come and let them go (as mine so recently did). Then, only when you are calm, allow your business—*whatever* you do—to arise from that tranquil core.

My mind objects: But maybe you'll sit there forever stewing and not doing another darned thing—and how could that be good? Well, it might be wise to take my own medicine, stop writing (the thing *I* am doing right now) and return to the stillness of being for a while. Yep, just noticed I have a tummy ache, a sure sign I am pushing myself again. So I will put down the pen, close the book and make room once more—if she'll have me—for the mystery of unearned joy.

November 24, 2004

Self-Care Is Calling

These morning pages of mine have become a habit. Was my guru right about habits? He said if we repeat a practice seven times in a row—yoga postures, or getting up to jog at 4 a.m., as he once had us doing—it would become a habit. Although I'm sure I made it to pre-dawn jogging more than seven times during my Kripalu visits, that one never made it close to habit status. But, if not always in a row, I've written for far more than seven mornings, and a habit *has* been born.

I don't buy the idea of seven being a magic number any more than I do the idea I should jog at 4 a.m. because the man in charge says so. (It could be that anti-authoritarian thing.) So yesterday when Rory the chiropractor challenged me to action (or really *in*action), I didn't take well to it. We were having our usual after-treatment chat in his funny little chiropractic office, the four patient tables lined up in a very public row behind a door that doesn't quite close. Rory was excoriating me for taking the prescription drug Celebrex to deal with my neck pain.

"Well," I cried with the chutzpa of a linebacker, "what would you have me do about this dreadful neck of mine—go to bed for a week?" Rory, who likes to have the last word in health care matters, pressed on: "Sure. If you knew going to bed for a week would get rid of the pain, wouldn't you do it?" "Of course," I shot back. Not to be outdone, he said: "Well, what are you waiting for? How bad does it have to get before you take drastic measures that might just work?"

He was right, of course. To ignore the body and plod on at all costs is the polar opposite of what I suggest to people in pain. Pain is there for a reason, the most compelling being to get us to stop and pay attention to the red flag it is waving in our face, or (as in one case I can think of) stabbing into the back of our neck. If a pain is so bad a person can say it's practically killing her and she takes heavy-duty meds to shush it, shouldn't she stop and give it her full attention? Duh!

It's perfect, isn't it? "Woman whose life and work is about listening to her body's signals so she can get to know, love and express herself—woman touting radical self-awareness and self-respect for the good of all—gets taken down by a pain in the neck, having refused to stop and attend to it, so she can write her damn book about it. You've got to love God's sense of humor.

If I were told I had cancer, as two young friends of mine recently were, I'd be right on it. It would be *do or die*. I'd drop everything to find the best doctors and treatment plans, resting up like mad in between all the research. If a doctor dropped the deadly "C" word on me, I'd listen up to this old body and its none-too-subtle promptings pronto. But a stiff sore neck? Not so much.

Come on, Suzanne. To be true to yourself and practice what you preach, you must more often do as you started to do this morning. After a good night's sleep you lolled in bed till eight. Now you sit writing quietly by the fire, wanting to let yourself rest in pure awareness, that spacious place— or *no place*—inside, where ease and love live, and there's nothing to be done.

You *want* to let yourself be, girl, but it's not happening at the moment. To come to ease seems to require effort today.

So here we go: I will direct my attention to how I am being with myself as I sit. I am uneasy, I notice, and I shift. How's my breathing? Not full enough. So I stop writing and exhale deeply a few times, opening my chest to receive each fresh inhalation. How am I *feeling*? I close my eyes and do a full-body scan, bringing my mind's eye and warm breath deep into my sore thighs, tight bum, and frozen neck. Okay. I am literally breathing myself to life now.

The more attention I pay, the more I feel how brutal I often am with myself. Not compared with a lot of people, I know. But it *is* brutal to keep ignoring my pressing physical and emotional needs in the interest of getting stuff done. It is brutal to move as quickly—as *automatically*—as I often do, without considering the effects of my actions on my vulnerable being.

When I stop dead to notice, I sense how tense I've been and how badly I need to relax. Can I ever learn to treat myself as kindly and gently as I'd treat someone else in pain? Might this be my true mission: to embody self-care—one tender, attentive inner and outer gesture at a time? Am I to become a living, deep-breathing elder model of supreme self-love, shining from deep inside out?

Help me, please, to understand that *what I do for myself, I do for everybody*. Practicing self-respect, even at the expense of a book or other overt service to humanity, may be the worthiest calling of all for me. If I can live what I discern and learn about profound self-care, the act of writing about it would be icing on the cake. *What bakes the cake is self-compassion.*

Help me, please, to understand that what I do for myself, I do for everybody.

Closing my eyes, I draw in another long deep breath. The fire crackles reassuringly, the cat purrs contently by my side. Although my physical pain may not be gone, when I am this good to myself it almost doesn't matter. In the dazzling light of self-love and care, pain is beside the point. Rory suggested that to me, now that I think of it, and his may be the most important point of all. As I begin to move slowly, *slowly* into my day, may even the slightest movement be made with consciousness—and yes, love—toward myself and my poor pain-riddled body first of all.

November 28, 2004

Silence vs. the Call of the World

Silence is deafening when we don't want to hear *the still, small voice within.* It's why lots of us keep the TV, radio or iPod constantly on. I know several otherwise normal people who can't sleep without the television blaring. But the same silence that can scare us to death—for fear of what we might hear were we to shut up and listen to ourselves—can be a golden opening into the heart and soul of us. My experience—both of fearing and hearing my inner voice—suggests we'd best *listen up* if we want to avoid being emotionally blindsided, as I was when my friend Lucy died and thirty years of a long-silenced Suzanne arose abruptly from the depths.

Unless it's forced out as mine was, the still, small voice within must often be coaxed out gently, like talking a terrified kitty down from a tree. Most of us so regularly spurn our inner voice that it may not trust us, nor we it, if we can hear it at all. To turn up the inner volume and really listen to ourselves, we must learn to turn a deaf ear to the siren call of the world, and get very quiet. We'll have to say no to noisy external demands—*and we must be willing to seem less kind.* When we do what we don't want to do just to make others happy, it interferes with the promptings of our soul.

When we do what we don't want to do just to make others happy, it interferes with the promptings of our soul.

We must learn instead to please only God, whose will is our will and whose voice is our true voice. That true voice is spoken through the stillness we can learn to discern in the pause between breaths and the gaps in our thoughts. Silence alone does not produce the stillness of grace. But if we attend to silence and cultivate its dark loam with awareness, self-love may take root, one soft, surrendered breath-space at a time. In this way, stillness creeps in to shore up the self against the raucous rocky ravages of a desperate ego-mind.

I am paying such attention as we speak, stopping, softening, opening my mind only now and then to receive the words sprung from thought. I open my eyes just when it is time to move the pen across the page. What a blessing Trond was called to Lebanon today, leaving me to take our anticipated family walk alone and in silence, and freeing me to make of these last many minutes a slow, sweet solo time for the soul. God bless us all, *God bless us all.*

November 29, 2004

Settling in with Maha

It is 6:30 a.m. on the first day of Pennsylvania's legendary deer season, not our favorite time of year here at the farm, where the deer we don't want shot abound. Trond is heading out to Lebanon to spell Bob while he hunts yet again. Having failed to bag a bear in that season, Bob is going after easier prey today. I could have gone hunting myself this morning, awake before five as I was.

I would like to realize once and for all that four, five or six a.m. are not the ungodly hours I have long and obstinately insisted they are. Dedicated yogis and monks of all stripes attest to it. And when I get up early like them and pay attention, I too get to discover that far from ungodly, the crack of dawn is God's time. It's the best time for Him to hunt me down and secure me, before the day lets my mind snatch me away like the easy prey I can become.

That's why it is also the best time for me to write like this, letting heart, hand and pen have me, letting myself surrender to God and the word, His will made manifest on the page. So here I am, ripe and ready to give up my resolve to God's, as I have begun to do with Maha on the phone, yielding myself to her so she can work her willful, wily ways with me.

I finally gave in and hired her for the full year of life coaching she insists on for her clients. Soon after we were official, she offered me a "reading." I am not a big fan of psychic readings, unlike a startling number of bright women I know. I was surprised Maha was into clairvoyance.

But this gifted French-Jewish artist-teacher-writer, once-model and all-round wise woman assured me it might help. Why not, said I, I who joke (though it's not altogether a joke!) that *I can use all the help I can get*. A reading might assist with my writing, both the doing of it and *what* to do with it.

Though the rest of the reading didn't yield much, the theme card Maha chose for me was an apropos reminder to "slow down and receive my life as the joy it is meant to be." The best thing about the reading was that I did it, this thing I am usually suspicious of—showing me I am ripe for what Maha has to offer. With her, and also thanks to her and her coaching prowess, I am taking on the role of student in a way I have rarely been open to doing since college. What a relief that I may now be humble—and confident—enough to again welcome learning from other teachers.

Although it has seemed arrogant, stupid and stubbornly self-defeating even to me, I have long been resistant to the role of apprentice. Improbably, I fought the influence of Ilana Rubenfeld, a strong European Jewish woman like Maha (and whom, like Maha, I admired), even as I was paying her big bucks, traveling far and working my butt off to learn to do her elegant work. But until this recent shift in my attitude toward Maha—and with the notable exception of Bapuji, and for a time Gurudev, who were in a league of their own—I've felt the need to protect myself from the possibility of other teachers' judgments, and from my own judgments about myself compared.

I have been afraid the teachers I emulate would see through me and find me less evolved and wise than I wish to be—and wish to be seen as. I felt that way with Maha at first. Already insecure with her before she asked if she could be my coach, I was anxious that as her client I'd feel worse than ever about myself. But the competition I created with Maha is over. Is it grace? Or are my years of being willing to feel painfully *less than* (when that is how I have felt) finally paying off? Have I burned up that karma at last? It may be a combination of the two, will and grace, *will and grace*.

However it came to be, I am no longer devastated to think that Maha, who is younger than me and I thought might be *my* client, may (as ego would have it) be a few points ahead of me on the enlightenment scale and able to mentor me. Far from looking down on me, Maha has shown love and a persistent desire to work with me. And that has been disarming, if not, I hope, too charming to my insatiable ego. Rather than feeling less than, I've let down my guard to welcome her as an ally and comrade-in-arms on the journey home to myself. What a huge and meaningful shift!

It helped that Maha had let down *her* guard to let *me* in—literally. Because her online scheduling system was too inflexible to work well for the likes of (I like to think) spontaneous me, it was often a hassle to set up our sessions—and *get in*. Though I told her that more than once, the problem persisted. I got so frustrated and annoyed with what I saw as her rigid control, I did something that, though easier than before, is still hard and scary for me: I confronted the authority figure I perceive her to be *head-on*.

Half hoping she'd get miffed by a power struggle and that would be the end of it—and of my need to look at myself again in the way good teachers force us to do—I gave Maha an ultimatum. I said that if I was only allowed to schedule during her limited hours on the three days a

week she coaches (and in her system, it's only in the first
and third weeks of the month for me, because my last name
begins with "G"!) then too bad; *I was out of the game.* I
waited with baited breath.

Fortunately for us both, my new coach passed my
inadvertent teacher's test with flying colors, by at once
letting go of having to have it her way. She replied with
the famous French phrase "Il n'y a que les imbéciles qui ne
changent pas d'avis!" (Only imbeciles do not change their
minds!)

While Maha asked me to *try* to schedule my calls in
her preferred weeks, she said she'd arrange to talk with
me whatever week of the month worked best for me. We
both won, and I was able to leave for our India trip with
that unpleasant matter resolved. And thank goodness. For
along with her insight and courage to speak hard truths, it is
Maha's normally cooperative, collaborative spirit I love. She
is the teacher I want to be—partner, friend and sister on the
way to the God we all are.

Out of the blue the other day Maha said she had good
news to share. "I've made a shift out of an old role I used to
play," she told me happily. "I call it The Miser." "That's great,"
I said, knowing she was right. Although neither of us said
so, I was sure my having asked her for more flexibility in
scheduling—and she having given it—helped precipitate her
more noticeably open attitude. We are both beneficiaries of
her surrender—from living in the control freak head, where
there is never *enough* (time, money or whatever we think we
lack) to the domain of heart, where plenty reigns.

I was genuinely glad for Maha, as if something
valuable had been given to me, too. And that was another
breakthrough for me. When people I admire have enjoyed

success, I've sometimes felt diminished and jealous of their accomplishments. I know in my head (and deep in my heart) that we are all connected and I *should* feel glad for them, but I don't always. This time with Maha,

When people I admire have enjoyed success, I've sometimes felt diminished and jealous of their accomplishments.

I did. *Her* spiritual advancement felt like *my* advancement as well. *I was able to share in her joy.*

What good news! My happiness for Maha suggests *my* miserly tendencies, which she had gently pointed out to me while acknowledging her own, may also be on the wane. How did that happen? We cannot force the sense of deep connection that allows us to feel others' victories as our own. We may *want* to be happy for them, and sometimes we manage to be, we lucky ones who've had the chance to form intimate bonds like I've felt with family, friends and fellow seekers. But until we can feel the pain and thus absolve ourselves from the *sin of separation*, we can't easily relish the progress of those who appear other (and more) than us. Their gain seems to speak of our loss.

It is only through compassion for our own dear beings that we come to feel the world as our family and to recognize that what is yours is mine too. Content with ourselves and our part, however seemingly small, we can stop comparing and proving ourselves to others. Secure in the knowledge of who we are, we understand finally that *there is no other*—I am That, *all* of that—which lets us revel in and with each other, no matter who seems to succeed the most.

Writing today, I feel gratitude as a palpable warmth and fullness in my chest for having called Maha forth to work with me. She showed up in my life because *I* showed up in my life, by saying a fearful *yes* to being guest leader of a coach friend's teleclass late last year. When Maha called in to take part, the door to our connection opened. Through such minor miracles, I am coming to appreciate my ability to attract what I need in order to grow. As Maha reminded me the other day, my capacity to do that is based on nothing more or less than living the love that I am. To be awash in love, to let it infuse and fill us till there is nothing but blessed bliss—that is all any of us has to do.

To be awash in love, to let it infuse and fill us till there is nothing but blessed bliss — that is all any of us has to do.

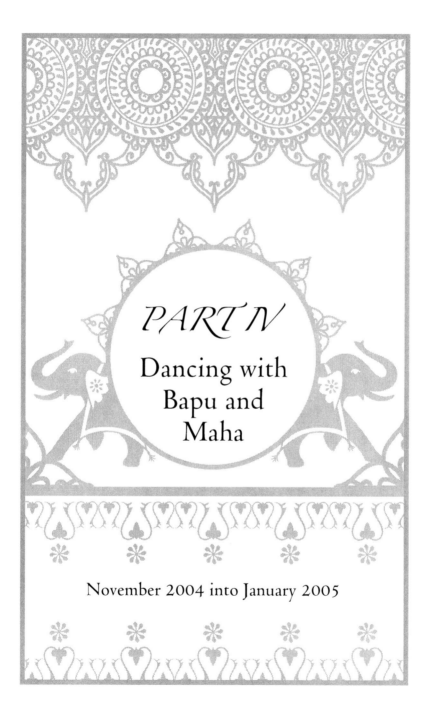

PART IV

Dancing with Bapu and Maha

November 2004 into January 2005

November 30, 2004

Being Bapuji Slowly

The writing continues, as I sit again on my cozy corner of the couch. The gray and white cat, inexplicably named Cider by an ex of Nora's—till we changed it to Umesh after a hotel butler we met in India—is curled up beside me. Like yesterday, Trond headed to Lebanon to deal with more engine problems. But unlike yesterday, this morning's sun, temporarily obscured by a cloud bank, was already up and out before I began to write. Thank God.

To receive my life as the joy it is meant to be are the words that come back to me now from Maha's card reading, like an assignment. I also remember realizing I must slow down if I'm to let joy in. But I am starting to see that slowing down may be a thornier matter than we think. When I think of *slowing down*, I think of not doing as much, keeping an open calendar, rushing about less. A slowed down me would leave time for things to come up unexpectedly, as they are wont to do in "real life" (which might better be called *reel* life, according to the spiritual masters who say life is no more real than motion pictures—a movie we make up from our running rampant illusions.)

I've been moving slowly—perhaps too slowly!—in the direction of winding down like that for several years. In the course of a day, I rarely have more than three coaching calls of up to ninety minutes each, with another appointment or two wedged in. That, which might be a light schedule for many people, would be a busy one for me. Does that mean I've slowed down? Not so much.

I can barely grasp the implications of a *real* slow down. Looking through the microscope Bapuji implored us to turn on ourselves and our behavior so as to help us grow, I see I can be doing very little and still be going fast and furious. Putting the brakes on my activity level is not enough. I can be as revved up as that old TV commercial Energizer Bunny, while sitting stock still, eyes closed.

If my mind is racing—as it often is—I am not slowed down, no matter how Zen-like I appear in the mirror. Since body and mind are one, there is no peace for the body until there is peace of mind. But what's the point of my coming to a dead halt? Why try to be like Bapuji, who sat still for years, slowed down so far he was *distilled* to an emanation of peace, radiant joy and love?

Since body and mind are one, there is no peace for the body until there is peace of mind.

Bapuji was amazing, but he was also an Indian swami, an anointed renunciate of the highest order, for God's sake. I am an American wife, mother, daughter, sister, life coach, writer, and so on. I have things to do—miles to go and people to please—before I sleep (or *wake up*). Aren't I inviting failure by emulating someone as different as can be from me? Why should I even try?

It is not a question of *should*, of course. I do want to be like Bapuji. I want to be as wide open to life as he was. In his presence, you could see how fully he took it all in, one juicy, usually joyous moment at a time. The joy and (when the situation called for it) sadness on his face was a delight to behold, and completely infectious. To let life in as he did, to receive and taste its bittersweet fruits, has got to be the point, if there is one. To live without letting life dazzle us—blow us wide open—is to miss the show, like a blind man gazing at the sun.

To live without letting life dazzle us — blow us wide open — is to miss the show, like a blind man gazing at the sun.

December 1, 2004

More About Being Bapuji

By pushing myself, and rushing blindly ahead as I still regularly do, I am cutting myself off from life around me and from the source of life within me, the abiding connection that alone can feed my hungry soul. We are starving here—I am and you are—cut off from the roots of our satisfaction by a terrible driving need to keep doing, having and being *more*.

I attack life, as my cat sometimes does me when I reach out to stroke him—reflexively, both of us biting the hand that feeds us. So how do I live an open, receptive, self-nourishing *Bapuji* life, without retreating completely into solo silence as the great swami did? And is that even within the realm of possibility? It's the question I keep coming back and back to. In coaching we call it an "inquiry" because it's a quandary so big, deep and knotty it keeps calling us to ponder it further.

Part of me says I know nothing about the answer. When I ask how to live like Bapuji, I draw a blank formidable as this page before words arrive. Another part of me, closer to my heart, says this: the last thirty years—almost half my life—have been no less than the quest for an answer to that question. And the answer is coming, not all at once as for some, but a little bit at a time.

Year after year, at what has seemed a snail's pace to this impatient ego-mind of mine, I've been making the arduous shift from fear-and-desire-driven living, with its great innate frustrations. And I've been moving toward a contentment I still usually realize only when I sit, as I am doing now, alone and silent like Bapuji; though as a matter of fact, I am saying these words aloud.

In the yogic scripture called *Sri Atma Gita* or "Song of the Soul," Krishna instructs his disciple Udaiva in the ways of spiritual development. During one of their most significant exchanges, Krishna tells Udaiva, "There are many ways to reach to the end of man's journey to God." But when Udaiva asks in reply, "I wish to know, Lord, the way that is best. Is each of these paths as good as the rest?" Krishna answers unequivocally: "The best way of all is devotional love." What a boon that is for me, who was born with the heart of a devotee.

A great wind, accompanied by a torrential rain, has just blown in. It's wildly whipping the locust trees around this old stone house and playing havoc with the thick green ivy covering the adjacent smokehouse. Just as suddenly, it all stops and a lovely blue sky starts creeping across from the west.

Whether we're devotees or simple sadhaks, *our* devotional love is likely to look as different from the swami's as a great storm does from a clear blue sky. But if we don't bow down to the Shiva Lingam as Bapuji did, we'd better find another worthy place to lay our weary heads, so our hearts may reign supreme. While traditional religious devotion may no longer be the most direct route to the divine (if it ever was), we'll do well

The Shiva Lingam, a black phallic-shaped stone representing the Hindu God Shiva, is a symbol for worship in Indian temples dedicated to that Lord of Transformation. You often see the lingam draped with garlands by eager devotees.

❖ ❖ ❖

to understand and practice the essence of its ancient self-subsuming rituals: *Thy will be done, oh Lord, not mine*—one way or another.

Thy will be done, oh Lord, not mine. That Christian mantra I often invoke is one way to turn our heads back to our hearts, where devotion lives. But it is only one. In order to know ourselves as love, we must each find our own devotional way. What sparks the heart in *your* chest? What warms and fills it round and full as the sun, which bursts forth from behind skittering clouds now, so bright that even inside the house I must close my eyes against its radiance?

Will I stay connected to my heart, radiant center of my being, while I get dressed, check email, and compassionately coach my first client of the day? I'd like to be able to do that, and to watch myself closely as I do, that I may learn and remember what it takes to keep me here now, as lovingly in touch with myself and others as Bapuji seemed to be. Slowly, slowly, Suzanne.

December 2, 2004

Relaxing into Love

Yesterday felt special because, even if I didn't always like what I saw, I succeeded in paying attention to the way I was doing what I did, how I was *being*, especially with myself. After writing, I checked email and got dressed, observing I was already scurrying a bit. I realized I had not left enough time to complete my morning routine before the first coaching call—*enough time* being a pretty basic requirement for the slowing down and taking things in I am aiming for.

I was feeling—if not necessarily acting—rushed, my mind moving so quickly it got ahead of my body. I couldn't keep up with myself, because my attention was already on to the next thing, rather than right here, now, *with me*. I (my mental self) was out of sync with me (my physical self), which kept me out of touch with my evolving needs, and so, out of sorts. I caught myself, and caught up with myself, during my first coaching call. Coaching is good that way.

Although the intent is to help clients catch up with themselves, coaching practically forces me to catch up with me too. For even if my focus shifts to my clients when I pick up the phone, the need to stay focused brings me back to myself. Coaching coaxes forth all of *me*—body, mind and spirit working in tandem—to bear on supporting clients. I'd been rushing, but I'd also just written about wanting not to rush. Committing to support my client helped me remember my commitment to myself.

After the call, and breakfast, dishes and laundry, there

was a long stretch yesterday when there was nothing I had to do. So what I did was nothing at all—but stop and attend to myself. Without the focal buffer of my client's concerns, I noticed that most of me was hurting like hell. So I did something I almost never allow myself to do. I lay down on this same couch where I now sit to write, and where I often meditate and make my coaching calls. And I allowed myself simply to *be*.

For two or three hours smack in the middle of a workday, I did nothing but breathe and feel, and breathe and feel some more (just what Rory wanted). Such a gift I gave myself! Twinges of guilt and doubt reared their ego-driven heads. But my pained body had had enough of the "You are not enough" story that keeps me up and at it at all costs— running about and putting out for its own sake, because *a good girl always should.* But now my body says: *I do, therefore I am* be damned!

I'd stopped, and I was lying there taking the time it took to reclaim the self beyond the doubting doer, for once paying little mind to Father Time. Instead, I was mindful of my body and vigilant about not getting mentally ahead of myself. I lay there, mostly awake even as I got more and more relaxed, which I did by doing Ujjayi conscious breathing. I used breath to tease my awareness down

Ujjayi is the basic yoga breathing exercise. In this practice, you tighten the inner muscles in the back of the mouth, as if to clear out phlegm, or hum. Working the throat like a kind of straw or suction pump, you draw the breath in and out through the nostrils in a long, steady stream. Listening to the soft wave-like sound that makes allows you to deepen and control the breath's flow. Some people visualize "healing light" and send it throughout the body.

❧ ❧ ❧

from my head into the bodily sensations mind labels as aches and pains.

The longer I lay training mind and breath on my sore parts, the more absorbed and relaxed I became, and the less they and I hurt. I know intellectually that attending to uncomfortable areas in this yogic way helps us stop holding them as painful, since *holding* is as much a mental construct as a physical one. That is what is meant by the expression *what we resist persists*, with its corollary that *what we accept dissipates*. Yesterday that familiar wisdom was my felt experience.

A few times as I lay there just being, my mind would let go of its grasp over the body. I'd let out a little inadvertent cry of release. This deeply tranquil state, where one is not asleep but the slate that is mind goes momentarily blank and frees the body, is what I think of as *Yoga Nidra*.

Yoga Nidra (yoga sleep), which I learned from my former guru Amrit Desai at Kripalu, has long been a favorite practice of mine. I have also encouraged my students and clients to try this simple rejuvenating technique for letting go. I was interested to see that Yoga Nidra has became a focus of Amrit's teachings at the Florida Amrit Institute, where he has lived and worked since leaving the Kripalu Center for Yoga and Health, in Lenox, Massachusetts.

❧ ❧ ❧

When we consciously let go—letting our minds go AWOL and our bodies soften—we let go into the source of life itself, which is to say love. With our guard down, we come to see and trust ourselves, so we can dare to do what we came to life to do: *to love and be loved in our own particular way*. Love cannot help but arise in us once we relax, since love is who we are when we let go of who we are not.

I've often guided or let myself go into the state of Yoga Nidra. What was new yesterday on the couch is that I let myself experience that relaxed, self-

Love is who we are when we let go of who we are not.

loving state for hours at a stretch. And though it's never been on any of my to-do lists, I realize only now that to stop, relax and recollect myself when I get lost is *the most important thing in the world for me to do.* Because to bring monkey mind back to dear body is to reclaim my spiritual power.

Thank you, dear God, for the pain that may set me free and return me to the love that I am. Please keep making me hurt, if that is what's needed to get and hold my full attention and turn my face toward You. I pray this physical pain won't last forever, but if it does, so be it. *Thy will be done, oh Lord, not mine.* Now it's time to step gently, attentively into this sure-to-be-challenging day.

December 3, 2004

Gratitude Meets the Miser

Finally a winter morning that is sunny and bright! Trond has gone back to Lebanon to tend to a downed engine. I am perched again in my writing place on the couch, bundled more toastily than usual as I wait for the heat to warm this big beautiful living room, and so, me. Trond, who is often up before five, stoically does without heat, which meant it was still damned cold when I got up.

As Maha said to me the other day, it is time for me to let go entirely of The Miser consciousness and to relinquish what she called "the fixation on what I am not." It was that fixation, of course, that kept me from being able to enjoy the success of others, as I am now learning to do. I must give up The Miser, she told me, so I may come to a sense of gratitude for all that I am—and all that is. For some reason, her suggestion brings to mind the *surrender* promised in my favorite *Sri Atma Gita* verse:

> *When you can surrender in full love to God,*
> *You'll rise to the heights of the heaven within.*
> *In blissful awakening, you will know your true self,*
> *And fathom the depths of the whole universe.*

Whew! You can't beat that for a promise. I feel the force of it in my body as I write the familiar words. But why did Maha's exhortation to greater gratitude make me think of this verse extolling surrender? Well, the more I can understand—*and appreciate*—that God and His love are alive in me, the more I can let go and awaken into the *Gita's* (and my) *true self*. It doesn't make logical sense to me. But I can feel it. Gratitude and surrender are two sides of the enlightenment coin, kissing cousins on the path toward universal love. You can't have one without the other.

Two interruptive phone calls later, and the warming light of gratitude still fills my being, an inner beacon calling me home to myself. I am starting to understand that to encourage gratitude is to invite surrender into the heart of me and so of *the whole universe*. For when I am grateful to God or to anyone, I am acknowledging that it is not all about *me, my* successes and *my* failures. That lets me lay my burden down—and be on my way to "surrender in full love to God."

Gratitude assumes I am not doing it alone, not holding the bag—or the universe—with my bare hands. The buck does not stop here. In a state of gratitude, I recognize there is someone else who shares responsibility and deserves credit for this clear mind, dear heart and sometimes luscious life of mine. The joy and relief of that helps me let go. When I know I am part of a whole that supports me— and am *glad* (which is also to say grateful) for it—I can give it up to God. The love source within gets a toehold, and the turtle gains ground on the hare that is my racing ego-mind.

I sit for a moment, felled by the grace of stillness, mind poised like my pen between thoughts. Do I write truth? (I ask again.) It's a question from mind, of course. The heart says yes, it is the truth I have written, stunning me into epistolary silence. I rest, temporarily suspended in gratitude's arms, thankful beyond words for this peace I feel, and for the love and letting go it speaks of.

I have been writing with more surrender, especially

today. Rather than thinking about what I might say, I stop and close my eyes. I wait, and wait some more. I am not as impatient or bored as I used to be, hanging out in the gap between words, which rise ephemeral as soap suds from a steamy sink. The gap is a real place, not an empty space. It may be richer and more compelling than the words, which if I don't write them right down can pop like those bubbles and be gone. The silent gap from which this language arises is a force to be reckoned with. But what is it?

If I had to name it, I'd call it the *ground of being—my* being—because it grabs and grounds me in the thoughtless, formless *is-ness* of life. It stops my mind and its normal thought stream in their tenacious tracks, until my grounded being has something it wants to say to me. This gap is an active state, rife with life, alert and relaxed at the same time. No wonder its words ring true.

I wonder whether *these* words that have arisen from the gap will make sense when I read them later. Maybe not. That will be disappointing to my mind and its eager ego, but less than it might have been yesterday, and that's promising. Whether it makes sense or not, I finally know that this mindless—or is it mind*ful?*—meditative writing, with its strange *being gaps*, is the only writing I want to do. Whether or not it's worthy of wider sharing, it helps *me* trust myself—and God.

I am back after breakfast, dishes, laundry and bills with more words on the way. I didn't write earlier as planned about Maha's assignment: *how to move while remaining still.* But I may have been practicing it while writing about the relationship between gratitude and surrender.

Here's a funny thing. On our last call, I boasted to Maha about stopping to nurture myself in the midst of a regular workday because my body hurt. She wasn't impressed. I was telling her proudly that, while lying on the couch—when I could (and to my mind, *should*) have been up in my office, say, soliciting business—I got a call out of the blue from someone I hadn't heard from in years saying she wanted to sign up for life coaching! How cool was that! Still Maha demurred.

I had taken Angela's call as a certain sign that listening to my body is all I need to do. Attend to the self, surrender, be grateful, and who knows what miracles can happen—Angela or another sort of angel may show up and move things along with little if any effort on my part. I was all psyched up about the idea of lying around more, in self-love. *But no.* It was okay to honor my body by stopping to rest now and then. The real challenge, though, as Maha reminded me, is to "stop the story" and *be still of mind, while still in motion.* No need to be lying around. But is she right?

Is *inaction in action* the highest path? To be in the world but not of it, out and about *doing* stuff without getting caught up in it? That's not what Bapuji did. In pursuit of enlightenment, he made a nearly complete retreat, with little worldly involvement except writing and now and then teaching disciples. It's true his motto was "love, service and surrender." But what did he mean by that?

I wonder whether we need to *serve* in the usual sense of that word. Is being actively useful in the world, however selfless and still of mind we are about it, the point? I don't think so. If Bapuji is any indication, enlightenment is the point: to move beyond the need to serve (or perhaps the need to be in the world at all), and simply BE. One who does that—and I keep returning to this—is of the utmost service without trying to be. The person we call *enlightened* is in service only to the soul, aligned with the deepest level of reality, where all is as it should be, and we all are one in the spirit. To the enlightened one, there is no question of service—no trace of *I* or *thou* left to serve or be served. When we are in full surrender, trust reigns and everything takes care of itself.

When we are in full surrender, trust reigns and everything takes care of itself.

At the same time that Maha urged the end of my Miser consciousness and a turn toward self-love and gratitude, she also told me she can feel how hard I've *tried* for love, both to love and be loved. "Leaving no stone unturned" is the way she described my prodigious efforts to recover the innocent, loving source from which I got separated as ego grew up in me, as it must in almost all of us. But have I loved too much and been kinder than I've wanted to be? Have I tried too hard, as Maha suggests, to be the good servant, relegating my own most urgent needs to the back burner?

Yes, I think I have. Maha is helping me see that fearing further loss of love, I have too often extended myself falsely to others and their causes, which are not always my own. I have bartered my personal power—which lies in being totally genuine, living from the true self alone—for approval, which is a poor substitute for love. Aha. I see that I am now writing about another thing Maha had recently invited me to look at: the relationship between my *power* and *kindness*, and how I might right the balance between those two potential adversaries in my life.

To be kind can mean to give fake approval, saying or doing "too nice" things to and for people for self-serving reasons, rather than as a thoughtful reflection of our inmost truths and desires. And that robs us of our authenticity and power. Of course there is value to kindness when it is a sincere response to circumstances that call for it. But not to put too fine a semantic point on it, rather than kindness, that might better be called *compassion*: situations when our hearts fly open in love to another, and all that we say or do with and for them arises from an inspired kindred heart.

Isn't *kindness* rather the fallback position of someone like me who tries too hard to be the good person, ideal life coach, and trusted friend everyone likes? And whom does that kind of kindness serve? If our power comes from living our truth and nothing but, aren't we all better served by our saying the honest hard thing and not the nice thing, or best, saying nothing at all? And so, may I *kindly* (but not too kindly!) proceed from the power of truth, rather than the need for love and approval, during my first call with Angela, coming right up. We both deserve no less.

December 8, 2004

Maurie's Epiphany and Mine

The gray morning dawns at last. I was awake by five, restless as ever. For more than an hour I lay in bed breathing and sensing my resistance to monkey mind's antics and their unsettling effects. I felt torn between trying to get more sleep before a busy day, and getting up early to write. I probably still felt guilty for not writing on Monday, when I was here alone with plenty of time.

Today, Trond is not in Lebanon but nearby, my coaching calls start soon, and I have lots to do before then. It's already Wednesday and I don't want to get too far out of this writing habit of mine. So, good time or no, here we go, at least feeding my hope that—through God's grace and Maha's support—I might share this growing wisdom of mine, perhaps by birthing a book.

Writing these words stops me in my tracks, throwing me out of my heart, where I had settled in along with Umesh. He's aligned himself along my torso, purring. And his little right paw, with its

> In fact, it was five years before I found myself editing the material I wrote that day, finally certain a book would somehow be made of it. As you will see, there was much more inner and outer work to be done to help me understand what I had here—and dare to share it.
>
> ❖ ❖ ❖

newly clipped nails, is adorably positioned as often right over the place where my heart beats. But mention of the book-to-be (or not to be) throws me back into my head, full of those same boring questions about whether it's time and whether I'm ready to go public through publication. Those very questions suggest I am not!

But Maurie is ready to go public. This dear client phoned first thing Monday to announce she's ready to *shout it out* that she's a life coach. On our call before last, I'd called her out for playing mediocre, when she's anything but. She got it and agreed to go that very weekend to a relationship coach training she'd been terrified to attend. Now having gone and done it, she is beyond excited to honor her path. Good for her. I may not have been acting as mediocre as Maurie feels she's been, but all this mediocrity talk is resonating with me, *about me*, and I'd like to understand why.

Maurie is a massage therapist, which is work she no longer enjoys, and she's dying to be a relationship coach. For years, I've seen and said I saw the powerful person she is, as she's worked my body with her warm, strong hands— the two of us chatting and informally coaching each other about the intimate stuff of our lives. I know Maurie is a born coach. Now she knows it too.

I was thrilled earlier this year when, at my suggestion, Maurie started coaches' training and hired me to mentor her. But until a week ago, she was hanging back, the cold feet of the "I'm not good enough" dance keeping her from stepping fully onto the floor. So she wanted me to be the first to know about last weekend's epiphany. Turns out she had showed up and spoken up in a group of experienced coaches and felt great about what she'd contributed and how she'd been received.

"I am a coach," she announced when I picked up the phone Monday morning. It was a statement of fact, her voice full of a confidence I had not consistently heard from her before. We both knew she meant it and that a career was being launched. I am delighted for her, and honestly, a little envious about her *aha* moment—really a series of moments that began on the earlier call, where we agreed she'd been hanging out in mediocre mode before she agreed to go train with the pros.

There'd been a dramatic few minutes at the end of that call, when Maurie recognized how even the extra weight she'd gained had been about making it seem okay to stay below the radar and be less than true to herself. "I feel I can keep playing small," she had told me, "because I look too big—too *fat*—to be fabulous." By her own account, Maurie is a "*fantastic* mediocre," way better at being fair-to-middling than most, and it is true she'd done mediocre well.

But "even fantastic mediocre ain't good enough anymore," she declared, right before committing to the training that had seemed impossibly intimidating minutes before. No more *settling* for her, thank God—and thanks to her courage, as well as (I'd like to think) the power of our coaching.

What does this have to do with me and honoring *my* path? For starters, I long for the kind of epiphany that saw Maurie get off our call and sign right up for that thing she'd been so wildly excited—and wary—about doing. The training was several states away and just a few days later. A single mother of two, Maurie is short on time and money. But the moment she *got* she was ready, off she went to do what she's here to do and get transformed on the way. How inspiring is that!

I want to be that clear about what's next for me. I haven't been since I saw Ilana Rubenfeld work her body-mind magic in 1989 and fell into a virtual swoon from the "gotta have it" hit I got. By the end of a week watching

Ilana work (the only time she came this way *and* that I ever attended the annual program where she happened to present), I'd signed up for two years of pricey weeklong trainings way north of far-off Toronto—forget a weekend workshop. So yes, lightning can strike me too. But do I have to wait for another bolt before I act as decisively as Maurie did?

And do lightning bolts always mean what they seem to mean? I'd say not, on both counts. Another *aha* meeting I had in 1996 seemed similarly serendipitous until the trail went stale. About the time I'd decided a book might be a better idea than the magazine articles I'd been laboriously trying to publish one by one, I met Toni Burbank over the coffee urn at a friend's wedding brunch. I don't drink coffee, but wanting to spell Trond on the long drive home—and with two Bloody Marys under my belt—a cup of Joe made sense. I couldn't believe my good fortune when I discovered who she was, especially since I liked her before I knew, and she seemed to like me.

The top editor at Bantam New Age, Toni had been the first to publish Deepak Chopra, was about to publish Daniel Goleman's groundbreaking *Emotional Intelligence* (soon to be on the cover of *Time),* and was one of the few folks on the planet putting spiritual books of my ilk on the map. Something big was afoot, I was sure. Having made that fortuitous connection, I was inspired to write a book proposal, which I sent off to her a few months later, heart all aflutter.

Toni read it, said she liked both my writing and what I was writing about, and offered to help me find an agent. Given the way it was going, I knew a book was on the way, until it wasn't. It might well have been had I persisted. But over the next several months, the process of trying to find an agent was chewing me up so badly I made the choice to give up, and I didn't look back.

Maurie won't give up. She is so *there*, and I may learn from exploring why. Maurie had her fruitful epiphany because she had waited a long time, smoldering away in mediocre mode while working up skill and courage to make her move. Ready as she was for ignition, a little stirring of the tinderbox was all it took to put her "suddenly" on fire. Her eruption was no more *sudden* than a volcano's. And so, I see, it may be with me and a book, years after my first failed attempt.

All the while, I too may have been in a state of preparation, but for what exactly? Could it be for a very different book—the one I am meant to write? This wouldn't be the *how-to* full of polished stories that Toni wanted, or the carefully crafted memoir my editor friend Meredith prodded me to do a few years ago. Could it be that the book I would do now, written like this as a raw unfolding process of self-discovery, might be a heart-opener on the order of Tolle's *The Power of Now*? It sounds insanely presumptuous even to me—especially to me—but those are the words that came.

I don't yet know. But if I continue to look deeply and use my writing to grow myself—if I continue to draw on Maha's keen intuition, trust, love and creative energy to inspire me—maybe, just maybe I'll be freed up to speak worthy words to the wider world in a really significant way. Maybe like Maurie, I too await only a final spark to honor *my* path by putting my growing down-to-earth wisdom and gift of gab together for the greater good. God knows that would be a relief.

Today I feel tired, doubtful and uninspired. But here's a thought that could fire me up: is it possible I can write without the spark of inspiration? Might I sometimes proceed from *discipline* instead? Maha says she does that. She, who represents for me the Perfectionist projection my Rebel has disowned, just gets it done, whatever it is. *So what if you're not inspired? Do it anyway* is what she'd say. We know that would be a huge turnaround for this girl whose mantra has been *do only what you love*—with the added implication of—*only when you'd love to do it.*

Could I really introduce more discipline and will into my life—I, the anti-authoritarian who has cherished Bapuji's surrender as the Way with a capital *W*? Wait a minute. Isn't that what I am doing today, making myself sit and write when I don't want to and feel yucky and unripe for the task (not to mention having to pee like hell)? Yes, I am disciplining myself to write when I am uncomfortable and can't see I have much of value to say, and that may have value in itself.

It's time to get ready for the first of three coaching calls. But I may have found my theme for next time: how I can dance in grace with the two seeming opposites, *will* and *surrender*. I have long felt most of us err on the side of will, pushing ourselves hard, little Sisyphuses with our big rocks. So I have advocated surrender, for myself first off. But my beliefs may be tainted by my rebellious perspective. I have wanted to do what I have wanted to do, and not what I didn't, all right. And when I am in that mode, discipline be damned! But maybe, just maybe, there is room for both.

How to be surrendered in action and do what I don't think I want to—to *will* myself to write, rather than always have to feel surrendered about it—*that*, Maha suggests in her stillness-in-motion assignment, may be my next mountain to climb. The Rebel alive and kicking inside doesn't like the idea of mustering more discipline one bit. But then again, what does she know? Maybe the right mix of will and surrender is the very match this tinderbox needs to ignite.

December 9, 2004

Will and Surrender

When I woke up this morning, a great idea I wanted to write about came right to me. Still half asleep, I didn't jot it down, and now, pen poised, my mind is blank as the page. I can't for the life of me recall it. But I feel softer and more in touch with myself than yesterday and that's a good start. If we want to express from our source, it helps to be in touch with Source, which comes to pass sometimes more easily than others. What's more, Source has to have something vital to say to us, if *we* are to have something vital to say. It's not entirely up to me how it goes here.

Yesterday, I felt out of touch with myself and Source but willed myself to sit and write anyway, for almost two hours. So it's not surprising I came around to the question of will and surrender and their mysterious relationship. I had thought of will and surrender as antithetical states—that you can't have one *with* the other, at least not at the same time, or maybe even much within the same person. You are either willful and disciplined, as I understand Maha is, or you are soft and surrendered, guided solely by soul, in the way I saw Bapuji to be. I thought I had to choose.

After yesterday, I am not so sure. Maybe *will* plays a greater part in *surrender* than I'd supposed. No question that to write from spirit I must be surrendered and connected to the heart and soul of me. But where does willful mind come in? Often from the get-go, I now suspect.

Maybe will plays a greater part in surrender than I'd supposed.

I assumed surrender happened of its own accord, and it can, overtaking me some days as a grace that leads me right to wanting to write. But on days like yesterday, when I was fighting writing, I seem to need to enlist my will—and its handmaiden discipline—to plunk me down to work. Then with any luck—or *grace* again—the willful act of sitting with pen poised gives way to surrender. Gradually I let go and sink into the spacious stillness of now, waiting, watching and allowing what is to come forth. I am guided toward the wellspring within from which this writing flows.

Whether I get here by will or surrender, the spiritual writing is itself a subtle partnership between the two. As I start writing, the mind, where will and rationality reign, must step aside so intuition can flower. But as feelings and insights arise from Source, to which I give myself over, mind must step back in, at least to turn the feelings to words. That dance goes on the whole time I write. A back and forth between mind and heart is what this writing is (and maybe much of life as well).

Yesterday was full of willful words and people, almost all day and evening long. Now, by way of balance perhaps, I am called inside to utter stillness. "Shush, shush, little one," is all I am getting…. "You have said enough…you *are* enough. Time to return to the gap."

December 13, 2004

Dying for the Love of God

I continue to question my path, asking myself way too often what the hell I am doing here and whether it brings me closer to heaven, a sure sign, methinks, that I am not enlightened. But who knows—and why do I care? My friend Jim, whom I met years ago and who wrote a book about enlightenment, thought I was enlightened right off the bat, God bless him and for what it's worth (and I don't mean that as a reflection on Jim so much as on our ideas about enlightenment!).

What is enlightenment but the title of a magazine I subscribe to? I suppose it's a name for the state where we know absolutely beyond the shadow of a doubt, out past the Valley of the Shadow of Death, that we are the world, the universe, the Alpha and the Omega, the immortal no-thing beyond and behind everything—empty, porous vessels afloat on a vast sea of love.

To be enlightened is to know and operate as much as humanly possible from the understanding that *Thy* will, not mine, is being done and that my life is happening exactly to the extent *I* give my will over and let it happen. Now again on this bright windy morning, words are coming through me like shafts of light through our old farmhouse windows. Am *I* the one writing? Yes and no.

My body sits here putting pen to paper as usual, but it is as if I am taking dictation. I am not thinking of what to say today at all. It is as if words, usually born of both heart and mind, are floating up instinctively from the fullness of heart alone, no mental intermediary needed.

Enlightened or not, I know I feel freest when I
surrender and stop trying to be or do anything, including
choosing which words to write. Yet I realize I also want to
be of service. And that speaks of *desire to do something*,
which doesn't sound like surrender, let alone enlightenment.

But *is* service *willful*? Or could it be more primal urge
than deliberate act—*to give
for God's sake?* Might it be a
basic human impulse, easy
and inborn as breathing,
to do what we can to
alleviate others' suffering?
Wild animals have no
idea of doing something

*But is service willful?
Or could it be more
primal urge than
deliberate act — to
give for God's sake?*

for approval or any *reason*—other than instinct. Still they
tend to their wounded and sick: the doe to her fawn hit by
a car, a goose to the mate with a broken wing, the gathering
elephants to nuzzle their dying and dead. They aren't being
deliberate; they are doing what comes naturally. Is it Maha's
inaction in action?

Yes. Maybe that's where I want to be after all, doing what
I must with utmost surrender, which is to say with love. So
here's this morning's burning question: How can I fan the
flames of devotional love—the highest of paths according
to the yogic scriptures I treasure—through the service I
am called to do? For this I must *surrender* altogether, being
willing only to step up, give up and give myself over to the
highest, purest, most humble and devoted place in me, even
as I am giving myself in service to whomever I may. Our
work must be a calling from deep inside out.

Here is my prayer: That I do my coaching and writing
without the least idea of how I am to proceed, without

needing to be anybody, as an act of love and sacrifice alone. To empty myself for grace is the task at hand—that I may bow down in darkness and ignorance and be lifted up in light. For the truth is I have no logical answers to my burning questions. Better then to let the questions have me, making ashes of a mind that wants and pretends to know what it cannot.

It is a different kind of writing I do when I am left by myself like this. These mornings on the farm with Trond gone to Nova Scotia, I am drawn inward almost automatically. My body is soft and alive, pulsing with effulgent energy, practically purring like the cat nestled next to me. Like him too, my eyes are pulled shut, again and again. I must keep forcing them open so I can write. These sacred mornings alone, my heart is a palpable, fiery force in my chest, more persuasive for once than my head, which seems content to sit at heart's gate and wait.

Nowhere to go, nothing to do but this, to swim in the divine stream, willing to drown in God's love, *dying for the love of God*. If, as Maha suggested, my heart was long ago broken—and my heart feels right now as if it was—then sitting and being in love is the calming balm that can salve it. Sit long and surrendered enough like this, the *Sri Atma Gita* tell us—and Bapuji lived and died (while in a state of Samadhi) to prove—and you "become the same as the God that you love."

This morning meditation and writing time I make for myself must be among the holiest of practices *for me*. How can I be sure to respect it? Whenever I can, I must make space for it, literally as well as figuratively now perhaps. Yes, it may be time at last to make ready the meditation space Trond built for me, so I can sit with God even when Trond is home. Will I make that big commitment? This is where the *will to surrender* comes in and the rubber meets the road. The good news is that the more I surrender through willful practice, the more I love to surrender and the less need I have for will. Cooperate with God and the path opens up before us.

For the third or fourth time this morning, the phone rings and distracts me—a bell to wake me up to the inner work still to be done? Until rings and bells disturb me not at all, I am

Samadhi or Enlightenment is the ultimate goal of yoga and meditation. Though there are many different stages and descriptions of the experience of Samadhi, suffice it to say here that it is a rare and blissful state involving the total absorption of the mind and consciousness of the meditator into Universal Mind or God. Bapuji apparently achieved and, toward the end of his life, maintained the state known as Nirvakalpa Samadhi. He died in India, sitting up while in Samadhi.

❖ ❖ ❖

not altogether free, not quite *enlightened* no matter what my enlightened friend Jim says. And so what? It's a word fixed in letters, and it's my choice whether to be fixated on it and fixed by it, or not.

I still feel the precious fullness arising from my heart. But it has been clouded by a roiling in my belly, where I felt that last phone ring as if it lived in me. I close my eyes again, or am *I* doing it? They want to close all right and do so willingly, but *I* have little to do with it. Expanding inward, I feel my breath deepen, opening my chest and gently releasing the tummy tension left from the ringing phone. A bird sings a sweet insistent song outside the window. The sound lands gently in my heart, creating no distraction from the peace that is gathering within me once again.

To be the peacemaker, and the ardent lover, is to offer the only true antidote to suffering and struggle—mine, yours and the world's. To sit like this, as Bapuji did for years, letting surrender replace mind's will—this is the path I am to follow above all else. To return to heart space as often as ever I can; that is my truest job, whatever else I do or don't do, as time rolls riotously on.

To stay present to heart's promptings I *must* slow down and rest in stillness. When I don't, I can forget myself—the peace and love that I am, and that we all are—in a New York nano-second. Then, instead of living organically, from love, I become a slave to the robotic motions of a conditioned life. The pull of mind is strong. To counter it requires an equally strong intention—the will *and* the surrender—to sit in mindless cultivation of a loving heart. That is what I do this long morning, and what I must do every morning I can. God knows, and I know, it's time.

January 3, 2005

Sharing Soul Food

This gray wintry morning is the first time I've been alone on the farm in the new year of 2005 and for the almost two weeks preceding it. The children—Teg, Heather and my adored grand boy Jasper—have come and gone, back to their busy lives, God bless them, leaving me here to face myself again. My blessings, not least among them these children and my honey of a husband Trond, are prodigious. But I am still learning to *count* my blessings and to let them relax and soften me, preparing me for the rest of my life and all that it may ask of me, the blessed one.

"I am being held" are the words that come to me now, the force of love and light in my life almost more than I can stand. Despite what I hope are my best efforts to let go into the flood of blessings, I feel myself withstanding it, tightening my muscles, even unto my heart, but against what? *True surrender* is the phrase I hear, the idea of which, let's face it, still scares me shitless.

To give myself over to God feels like the ultimate sacrifice—like death. To let reality *really* shape me is what I say I want. Instead, I hole up in my head and hold out against being fully held, even sometimes by my devoted husband who rubs my feet and gives generously of himself.

How to break this will of mine to be a separate somebody, when I know well that to be nobody (or be *willing* to be) is the way to truth and light. At this rate, 2005 already three days old, I will be *no body* all right, before I know it. We are dying here, all of us, while I continue

123

clinging to frivolous desires for recognition, as if to life itself. Another Christmas has come and gone, in a flash I tell you, and here I am still anxious and regretful for what I have not done—*dared to expose myself.*

What do I mean—*dared to expose myself?* I mean to relax my guard entirely, to open the gate made by my mind— that others might rush the inner sanctum, plunder the family jewels and eat the sweet fruit of my ripening soul. That's what. To be of such exhaustive service, I must truly forget myself and all that *I* would be and do. I must turn myself in and turn myself out, letting God have me for purposes known only to Him. I must stop trying to know what I am to do. For God's servants, there are no five-minute, let alone five-year plans.

I mean to relax my guard entirely, to open the gate made by my mind — that others might rush the inner sanctum, plunder the family jewels and eat the sweet fruit of my ripening soul.

We who would serve souls must wake up and pray, my way to pray being through these words I write. We must let go and let God. How? By coming back any which way we can to the fortress of body-mind, scaling the moat and breaking down the walls, brick by brick—one conscious breath, one written word, one spoken mantra, one meditative moment at a time.

We must keep choosing heart over head, soft over hard. We must opt for this exact moment—*now*—however painful, over ruminations on past victories or dreams of future glory. We must pray "Thy will be done, Oh Lord, not mine" over and over again until we *get* it so well we can *give it up*—to

God. We must be willing not to know, and to be led through endless darkness, guided by faith in nothing more than the candle of "I am that I am," in this moment and the next.

Oh, this no-path takes courage, the willingness to burn and burn, till there is nothing left to will or want but love, till mind is totally subservient to heart. Rather than stifle mind, we must feed heart's fire—the surest, kindest way to starve our will. Rather than slap the hand reaching for the cookies (or wine) we must learn to offer a hand—food and nectar for the soul—to our famished, thirsting selves.

> *We must feed heart's fire—the surest, kindest way to starve our will.*

As I write those words, I notice my left hand gripping tight this book where I write with my right hand, which like the left also grasps (the pen) with all its might. I'd be surprised if I hadn't already noticed myself waking up with clenched fists on many recent mornings. How can I lend a hand that's all balled up? How can I share a heart that's gripped by fear? I must let go. I must.

Yesterday, I wrote an inspirational email to 200 people. I told them I've been learning to honor and love myself, so I might love them, my life and all it brings. That's been my way these last thirty years since Lucy died and helped me be born again (not in Christ but in love—on Valentine's Day, no less). And it's true I have not stood still. I was a *ball* of tension then, my fists and all of me taut as a drum. Lacking example or experience, I had no hint at first of how to free myself from the stranglehold. Till I remembered yoga, I was at a total loss about where to begin.

Since then, Bapuji's example and my own experience, with yoga and much more, have taught me something about how being with ourselves attentively, softly, *lovingly* as possible, can free us for God's will. And I have learned that God's will (what God and life want for and of us) is always of greater service to humanity—not to mention our own soul—than what *we* think we want.

So please, dear God, show me who I am beyond every idea I might ever have had about myself, for then and only then will I want what You want, what is right and good for everyone. Sitting here, writing from heart and not from mind, is about as right as it gets for me, connecting me as it deeply does to my breath, my body-being and my soul. Here, now, my mind is reduced, or should I say *elevated*, to its rightful role as handmaiden to the glory that I am—and we all are.

Returned to its proper place in the scheme of things, mind is no longer the ruler, but finally the subject of the *I* that is also *you.* Thus are we connected to all who suffer, the starving survivors of the recent Asian tsunami and the soul-selves of the hundreds of thousands of innocent children and adults who were lost in a flash (flood). May God bless their restless souls, and bless us all!

PART V

Bliss, Love and a Big "So What?"

January 2005

January 4, 2005

Happiness or Bliss?

I successfully avoided putting pen to paper till almost noon, not normally the monks'—or my—most contemplative hour. I was painfully aware of what I was *not* doing, guilt licking away at the edges of my consciousness like our thirsty cats at their often empty water bowl. I lay in bed till past nine, listening but paying scant attention to the second side of my worn *Sri Guru Gita* tape. Those favorite heart-rending verses almost always pull me back to center, but not today.

As willing as I was yesterday to sit, be and write is how unwilling I am today. While I begin to settle back into myself, I feel my self-judgment as a kind of heartache, literally, in the left side of my chest. Even as I watch my mind sniff out trouble—any trouble will do (and isn't there always something if we sniff around long and hard enough?)—I know how much I have to be glad for.

God knows I want to focus on the grace, attending to the light and lovely in my life. I want to be happy and to hold happiness as an intention. But a "Happiness Index" test I took online the other day verified that I have a way to go in that last department. After I answered a bunch of basic questions, the index was programmed to inform me that, while I am pretty happy overall, I don't concern myself enough with *staying* happy, keeping up the good work of happiness, so to speak. In the matter of happiness maintenance, I got my lowest score—six out of a possible ten.

Now that I think of it, though, that may not be such a bad thing. As Osho reminded me yesterday in his book, *India My Love*, happiness is on the same pendulum swing as its sister feeling, *unhappiness*. Happiness lives only in contrasting relationship to unhappiness. While I am more than willing to be happy when happiness comes to me naturally, to try to *stay* happy may be to invite in equal measure unhappiness. Do I want to put myself in that position?

> **Osho**, also known as Bhagwan Shree Rajneesh, was an Indian mystic, author and spiritual teacher with an international following. He moved to America and lived a mighty strange life. His teachings are published in his many books, which I was surprised to find lining the shelves of my guru's study during a period in the 1980s when we worked together briefly on a book Amrit never published. Maha is also a fan of Osho, which, given how radical they both are, is no surprise.
>
> ❧ ❧ ❧

Happiness and unhappiness are okay according to Osho. But to transcend them is to open ourselves to bliss. Bliss, he writes, "is without any opposite to it. It is serene, tranquil, cool. It is ecstasy without excitement," an idea I am beginning to appreciate.

Bliss, it seems to me, is what's there when there is nothing else going on, as I like to say about love. For like love, it's what remains of us when we stop identifying with and reacting to the hot swirling world of sense objects and off-the-wall emotions we attach to them. To know bliss, we must learn to sit and watch mind's grasping with calm—and yes—all the *cool* we can muster.

We don't need to intellectually grasp the *reasons* for our mind's grasping, though plenty of authentic seekers try to do just that. What I am talking about is noticing what grasping *feels like* (no matter its object or objective)—in the mind, yes, but especially in the body. We must get still enough to detect when thought ripples disturb mind's naturally clear—which is to say *blissful*—surface. And we must feel where and how those ripples make waves in our body, *so we can use the relatively concrete feelings body provides to release what is blocking the bliss.*

Now for instance, I'm aware of a spasm in my colon. Diversionary as it might be to do so, I have learned that it will not help to identify *why* the spasm is there. I could think about it and figure out what's bothering me, but for what? Getting to the root of the discomfort in my mind would still leave me in the realm of…well, mind and its ideas. And until ideas become our *felt experience*, they are just that, mental cloud forms too insubstantial to transform us—or to be transformed—though they sure can affect us. I cannot *think* my stabbing stomach away (or I don't *think* I can!).

If I want to be transformed for bliss, or even plain old happiness, I need a more substantial approach than analysis. I must close my eyes and deliver my mind and the full weight of my attention over from the realm of word-thoughts to the world of physical phenomena. I must face and embrace my tummy ache, wishing it well, not with ideas—of where it came from or how I might right it with right thinking—but with warm breath and openhearted loving awareness.

I must *be fully with* the part of me that manifests as tight, sore, sad, or whatever it is. I must bring all of me to bear on it, and I do. By accepting myself and my "wound" as best I can—not in concept only but in all its raw physicality—I accept myself *just as I am*. That frees me better to accept others as they are, and all life as it manifests, ripening me for the possibility of bliss.

I may not be in bliss this morning. But I am here now, more present, willing, surrendered and patient with myself than when I began to write. I *hurt* less in body and mind. Though I am not happy, I am less unhappy than I was. I haven't transcended those two emotional opposites to realize bliss today, but neither do they have me by the throat. We'll take what we can get.

Yesterday I felt what I dare say *was* bliss, as I lay listening to my less favorite opening verses of the *Sri Guru Gita*. After that I wrote until I felt done with drawing words from the bliss place. At noon, late for me to get going virtually, I fired up the computer and discovered several strong testimonials to the work I've been doing as a life coach. They came unsolicited, an unexpected response to the mass emailing I had sent out about what I am up to. The appreciative, laudatory expressions, from two current clients in particular, touched my heart and made me glad.

Though my response to kind words may have been tinged with bliss, I think it was mostly happiness I felt. It was brought about by and dependent on other people telling me things I want to hear, food for the ego as well as for the soul. Nothing wrong with that except, as we know, happiness, like emotions of all stripes, is fleeting. Firing up my computer this morning, I found no more personal accolades and was not so happy about that. But I was not so unhappy either, which suggests that in my movement toward the (cool) bliss department, progress may be underway.

January 5, 2005

Odier's and Our Tantric Quest

It's another gray wintry day, but today, instead of heading for the plant as he's done the last many days and was supposed to do today, Trond is home. I was surprised to find him set up before the bright crackling fire, computer on his lap and coffee in hand, when I emerged from upstairs thinking myself alone—and ripe to write in my usual solitary way.

Can I be as honest with myself and go as deep while he's in the room as when I am here with only the cats? We'll give it a try. Trond or no Trond, my heart says I am more self-connected today than yesterday. The sense of heart's presence in my chest is so intense I almost ache with it.

Oh, dear heart, what is it you want of me? I wait…. I listen…. It's always the same thing, isn't it: that I stop, get still and give myself to you. *That* is what the Tantra doctor orders in Daniel Odier's stunning work, *Tantric Quest*. Throughout the book, which I've been devouring, Odier's teacher, an enigmatic Tantric master he meets in the Himalayan forests, offers him the most stirring guidance I've ever read about the path to freedom. Her wisdom and

> **Tantra** is an amalgam of practices which may include yoga and chanting. Though its intent is to use the material world as a means to both enjoy and transcend that very world, Tantra is often misunderstood and promulgated in the West as a series of sometimes bizarre sexual practices.
>
> ❖ ❖ ❖

his have affirmed and deepened my understanding of what it takes to be a yogi, or in my case, yogini: in a word, *heart*.

The Tantric master's teaching is pure and simple, and it is only this: *meditate on the heart*. Forget the yantras, mantras and ascetic practices pursued by yogis of yore—and of late. Leave gods and gurus behind. Only stop and sit, stand or lie, whichever pose you like, and attune to your heart.

That is Tantra's fundamental practice and only requirement, according to Odier. It feels right. When the heart is whole, and we are wholly *with* it, we are holy. Higher and lower chakras stuck in inertia or pain start to spin toward healing the moment the heart is glad, or in Osho parlance, *blissed* (the made-up word that came to me, and is appropriately close to *blessed*!).

Weeping as I read, I've felt Odier's words transform me, pulling me deeper into *my* truth. Beyond the simple focus on heart and the love it foments, he affirms what I've long sensed: that the surest way to freedom from the fire of worldly desire is to step *not* back, as many would have it, but right into the fire—*of worldly desire*. Yes! We must show up for the reality dance bare-naked and let the world consume us. The way *out* of the mire is to wade deep *in*.

> *We must show up for the reality dance bare-naked and let the world consume us. The way out of the mire is to wade deep in.*

To release desire we must enter into it fully, steeping ourselves from head-to-toe in the love and lust, the pain and ecstasy, the disappointment and whatever else a human life of the senses presents. We must come to the game wholehearted, whole-bodied, ready for joy and destruction.

So, dear one, re-*member* your heart. Let it have you as you jump in with both feet to pursue the desires religions eschew. Soon nothing will touch you—no, everything will, but nothing will *hook* you. Dive into life and be free. That's what I took from Odier's book and will give my best shot.

My tears were nothing less than the joy of recognition and relief we feel when we meet with truth: I am enough, and if I *suffer and enjoy life* enough, the egoic *I* must burn, dissolve and disappear altogether in Shiva's transforming, encompassing arms. *I* will be here and not here, all at the same time. I will know my heart as your heart, the heart of God—reality itself.

This is great. It's what we human beings are born to do. What else? To live our lives as embodied love unfolding. And to deliver ourselves squarely into life and love's arms, we have to traverse the pathways of whatever unloving and unlovable—which is also to say *untrue*—motions and emotions *lie* (in both senses of the word!) along our way. We must recognize that the feelings we disdain and dismiss as "all-too-human" are the rose-petalled path to divine grace in disguise.

We must recognize that the feelings we disdain and dismiss as "all-too-human" are the rose-petalled path to divine grace in disguise.

What a strange notion, and spot on. Of course, we must know and embrace everything if we are to let everything go. *We can't let go what we haven't let come*, as I like to say. Without awareness of it—whatever *it* may be— we can't access it. How can we release our grip till we get

135

a grip, not in the sense of taking control, but the opposite, by grokking and giving into our feelings fully?

Angst, anger, jealousy, shame and blame: these ugly relatives—all children of fear—are the doorways into the heart and its inner sanctum, love. Until we are willing to enter equally into experiences that might provoke our most dreaded feelings, love and its sister bliss will necessarily evade us, if not avoid us altogether. We may glimpse them for moments at a time, but they will not be established in us or us in them. Until we can welcome fear as the other side of love's coin, and as a part of us (when we feel fearful), we stand in constant danger of fear pushing love aside and leaving us—where else?—in fear and the pain it causes, far from love's sheltering arms.

All this I have known in a way for a while. But thanks to Odier's book and the writing I have just done here, I now know better the truth of these words I have often said: *feelings are the voice of the soul.* To realize soul's bliss, the *heart,* which is home to these soulful feelings of ours, must be our mother, father, guru, lover and friend. Let us treat her like the *Feelings are the voice of the soul.* beloved kinswoman she is, listening to her subtle murmurs and giving her all the respect she deserves. That's a sure way to command the respect *we* deserve, from ourselves first and foremost. This is what we mean when we say that to know and love our self *as is* is all we ever need to do.

January 6, 2005

Happiness and Unhappiness

I am alone again this morning except for the yellow cat, Arba, whose new Indian moniker, Bhagul, hasn't stuck. Despite my ardent admonitions, he is happily lapping water from under the Christmas tree, which I insist on keeping up and will now have to water again. Trond is back at the plant, leaving me with a whole day by myself, to myself and of myself, without a single appointment. There's still no hint of sun, and a gray chill fills the air inside and out.

Today, dependent as I tend to be on what's out there (and I don't mean only the weather), I am unhappy. And I'd best be making a practice of welcoming or at least accepting it. How? As usual, the trick is to be with it (if not to welcome it), attending to its unpleasant manifestations in the body. My unhappiness, I can't help but notice, is making me sick to my stomach. So if I am to take my own medicine, I must take my mind—and the not-so-dazzling light of my present awareness with it—down into the pits of me, where I am so upset I have started to gently burp.

As my awareness travels down, I notice a sudden sharp sensation in my chest just by the heart, which distracts me from my gut. Dear God, please help me be with this all too visceral discomfort my head is in the habit of creating. Help me focus this mind of mine on feeling and healing the pain it causes with its less than charitable thoughts. I close my eyes. I take a huge breath in and blow it forcefully out. Tears appear, clearing the sour inner air for a minute, but only a minute.

The tummy ache gets a grip again, prompting a loud emission out the mouth. I know this unhappy gut-level feeling well, as the pain of "not enoughness," cloaked today in the guise of disappointment. While it may not help to know why I feel this way, I do know, so here it is.

Years ago when I was a Kripalu disciple, I was honored to have been asked by a respected senior disciple, Jyoti, to document in writing the last time Bapuji sat with us, his American spiritual grandchildren, before he returned to India to die. The piece I wrote about that special day was published in the Kripalu journal, edited by my dear friend Dennis. But even though I've had Atma's book about Bapuji for a while, I just realized my story could have been—and to my mind should have been—but was not included there among the many disciples' reflections about him. Boo hoo.

The ego lives for recognition, and to the extent I continue to live in—and out of—ego, there is never enough of the stuff it needs to feed on, to fill its gargantuan gut (thus upsetting my own). The happiness of recognition one day is followed by a desire for acknowledgment the next, and by *unhappiness* again when more kudos are not forthcoming. This dependence for my happiness on what drops in from outside is a tough nut to crack (and perhaps not so different from *crack*).

The only nutcracker I know is my willingness to sit, feel and wait for the shift to grace that returns me from mind's grasp to the self fed not by others' noisy praise or blame, but by the still, small voice within. For now, though, my mind is a force to be grappled with, as it fights my body for control. It's got me by the belly and is grabbing for my heart, the better to block the love that alone might overcome it. Who is winning? Who knows? Though I'm less *unhappy* now, I feel weak, tired, unsure and insecure. All this I must welcome.

Having stirred the fire and added a log or two, let me close my eyes and be with myself as I am. To drink sweet liquor from its source I must be patient and still. Give me the courage to sit in the quiet and wait some more. My attempts toward the light feel feeble, my patience thin. Even so, my heart quickens. Thank you for whatever measure of divine nectar you feed me, unworthy of it as I may (or may not) be. The slightest taste of amrit is a world beyond the fleeting drizzle of happiness that might have come from appearing in the Bapuji book.

The fruit born of the heart, and the juice distilled from it, is always and forever. However hidden, it lies waiting within, ready to burst forth sun-like to warm us whenever we play God and move the inner clouds aside. To know bliss we must forgo happiness and the shortcut it promises to fulfillment of our longing. We must let happiness come and go, just as we gladly do unhappiness, while we indiscriminately practice non-attachment wherever desire and repulsion show up.

> **Amrit** means divine nectar in Sanskrit. Yogis say that one can actually taste the sweetness of God, much as one might see a heavenly vision or hear holy choirs. I have had none of these sensual spiritual experiences, and speak metaphorically. But it may not be a coincidence that I am drawn to this lovely word, as the given name of my longtime spiritual teacher, Amrit Desai.
>
> ❖ ❖ ❖

We must kiss even bliss goodbye at such times as she decides to return us to our less than blissful devices. Who are we to orchestrate our lives? It is our job only to surrender so fully that we may discern the divine order and play our part. Let the master puppeteer produce her play—the *divine* play—and let us do her bidding, with all the strings attached!

It is our job only to surrender so fully that we may discern the divine order and play our part.

It's ironic that when I get anywhere near the place where I *get* that and know I am not the doer, I no longer give a shit if anyone wants to publish my stories, or even *gets me*, which used to be my primo *raison d'être*. But I see I am not free of that desire now. I've just reread what I wrote here, found it lacking, and now that I'm thinking of turning my journal into a book, wonder again if it, if *I*, am good enough. The painful old question persists. So be it. (But better *not* to reread perhaps.)

140

January 8, 2005

Love Letters—Thich Nhat Hanh's and Suzanne's

After yesterday's pink Eastern sky promised a sun we never saw, it's the grayest of days, pouring cats and dogs to boot. Trond said it rained hard all night, and, ear-plugged as I was, I'll have to take his word for it. But darn it, the Pennsylvania Farm Show started this week, which means it's supposed to snow! Enough of this icebreaking, and on to deeper, hotter stuff while we have time.

This morning while reading *Taming the Tiger Within: Meditations on Transforming Difficult Emotions* by Thich Nhat Hanh, I was stopped by his suggestion that the love letters we write can change not only the people we write them to, but through them, the larger world. As he wisely points out though, before our love letters can transform another, they have to transform us. "The time you take to write the letter," he says—and this is what hit me—"may be your whole life."

> **Thich Nhat Hanh**
> is a Vietnamese Zen Buddhist monk, teacher and peace activist who lives in France and has written some 100 books, many encouraging the practice of mindfulness.
>
> ❧ ❧ ❧

My throat caught and my tear ducts swelled as I read Thich Nhat Hanh's metaphorical words. I was moved when I realized *I* am writing a love letter, right here, right now, these raw words of mine telling the story and representing the living, breathing process of a life unfolding unto love, with the added purpose of sharing that love as widely as I can. As Hanh suggests, love is an experience we can inspire in others only to the extent we've been felled by a blast of it ourselves.

My reawakened client and early yoga student Lauren came to a similar realization in yesterday's coaching call. Reminding herself of the importance of self-care for the wife and mother she is, she came around to a favorite notion of mine: we can only give to others what we already have ourselves. How right that is. It has been thirty years and counting—half a lifetime—since *this* wife and mother woke up. Half a lifetime has come and gone since I started preparing a love letter by learning to love myself, one day at a time. For the less-than-half-a-lifetime that's left me, the beat goes on, as I seek to turn myself—and my every last nasty emotion— back to Source love.

We can only give to others what we already have ourselves.

We know I can still doubt if I'll find the will or the way to gather, type, organize and actually *send* my love letter. But as my doubts play out on the page, and on the sore, tired battlefield of my body—lately in my queasy gut—the struggle they create is weaker. I feel blessedly less invested in success, suggesting that the love transformation I want for humanity is alive and moving in me. Maybe I *am* ready to do this, to shape and share with the world what I've been doing for me—so *others'* struggles too may be less, my love letter flying in the face of all our fears.

I suspect it is as hard for many people as it has been for me, to sit in the dark with scant sense of light at the end of the tunnel. A glimmer or two may be enough to sustain the heartiest and most faithful. But some of us want the guiding hand of a mentor. Why *not* call out for help from one (like me) who has parsed the available maps, stumbled, picked herself up, run into and wrestled to the ground the demonic egoic emotions that would stop the gods in their tracks?

Like the rest, I have pressed on through the diminishing gloom—in life and on the page—so I think I can be trusted on this: the light that's been dawning in me is alive in us all. I can hardly wait to show you!

The light that's been dawning in me is alive in us all. I can hardly wait to show you!

January 10, 2005

"So What?" at the Farm Show

It's been forty-eight hours since I wrote. That's because Saturdays are either errand or play days, and I don't work Sundays unless you count vacuuming, desk catch-up, un-decorating a holiday bedecked house and sundry other tasks, which is how I spent yesterday. But Saturday was all about recreation and I surprised myself by holding up under pressure and having fun to boot!

I've never spent so long or had such a romp at the Pennsylvania Farm Show. Going with our adorable Nora and her boyfriend Jack helped me stay with the program and enjoy it. My increased physical and emotional stamina were nothing to sneeze at either. I am a heartier woman inside and out, even as my arthritic body aches and pains me more than ever.

My legs are strong, and the lungs that power them too. After years of strength training and treadmill walks, not to mention the ups and downs of getting around the Himalayas at more than 12,000 feet, the once-challenge of the Farm Show experience was a piece of cake—of the yummy Pennsylvania Dutch *funnel* variety. As we traversed the twenty-seven acres (all indoors, once you make it in from

> **Funnel cake** is a Central Pennsylvania goodie made by pouring batter through a funnel into hot oil in a circular pattern and deep-frying it until golden-brown. Often coated with powdered sugar, it's a popular treat at ballparks, carnivals and festivals, and it is as delicious as it is fattening!
>
> ❧ ❧ ❧

the distant reaches of the vast parking lot), I kept up with the best of them.

I used to be impatient when, during Farm Show breaks from ogling cows, chickens, draft horses and pink soporific pigs in the barns, we'd settle down on bleachers in the large chilly demonstration arenas. This year we sat as usual, watching streams of more—or often, *less*—skilled riders gallop round and round the dusty ring for this competition or that. Nora the horse vet was enthralled, but not I. Still, tedious as it got to watch the umpteenth cowgirl jump off her horse to try to rope a goat in record time, I was unruffled where once I'd have been crabby.

The Farm Show was no more scintillating than usual this year. But as I said to Lauren the other day about something that was bugging *her*, "So what?" The Farm Show is the Farm Show and for some reason, or maybe no reason at all, it no longer bothered me to spend an entire afternoon traipsing about there. As I'd reminded Lauren, "So what?" was a phrase our former guru picked up somewhere to help us lighten our load around how *things s'posed to be*. I use it with clients and myself to this day, and when you can get your mind around it, it's a pretty liberating pair of words.

Your husband called you a bitch (as Lauren's has)? *So what?* As in "*So what* does that have to do with you?" or "*So what* the hell does he know?" or "*So what* do you want to do about it?" Or just plain old "So what?" as in "Who cares?" He's an idiot and it's not worth fretting about. There are lots of rich, rhetorical follow-up questions if you take "So what?" and run with it. Mostly it's an impish way to help us let go of judgments that cause us to kvetch and retch. Judging from this year's Farm Show, my "So what?" quotient is up, cause for this girl to do a little happy dance.

How great not to take things so damned personally—and so seriously. As recently as last year, I'd have felt

How great not to take things so damned personally — and so seriously.

our six-hour Farm Show expedition was an awful waste of my precious time. Not significant enough for a "spiritual seeker," you know. This year, it was simply what we were doing on Saturday. Far from put off, I was able to revel in the bustling hordes, sweet smelly animals, and those fried mozzarella balls, and I was barely bothered by the arena's loudspeaker so muffled we missed much of the commentary that might have made the endless rodeos make sense.

It was mostly better than fine this time, I suppose, because *I* was fine. How I am with myself wherever I am, whatever I am doing is what counts. It's not *where* I am, it's where *I am*, the state of my being always the crucial factor. If I feel grateful and glad in myself, then all is well with the world. If not, the same world can suck and seem to suck the very life out of me.

You should damn well be grateful and happy, Suzanne, my at-the-ready mind rebukes me a few minutes later. You are blessed and then some. There is nothing sucky about your situation, lucky girl. All right, and true enough. If all I had were one roof over my head (I've got several), the clothes on my back (I've got closets full) and enough to fill my belly (I am ever too full), I would have it made compared to the recent tsunami survivors and practically everybody everywhere.

But my good fortune goes well beyond roofs over my head, clothes galore and a stuffed tummy. As Dennis once said to me while I agonized over some choice to be made, my life is "an embarrassment of riches." He is right, and I *am* embarrassed. Not by the relative riches, which, as a privileged middle class American, I was born to, but by the stunning reality that it is taking most of a lifetime to revel in my riches—to grow up and into the abundance within and around me. I may have it all, but relaxing into and appreciating all I have is another matter entirely.

To say I'm not relaxing and enjoying my life doesn't touch my sorry thankless state some days. I can get crazy as if a tsunami were upon me when, say, I have to make a near impossible left turn out of the parking lot of my wonderful women's gym into rush hour traffic. Or when I get behind some poor slow driver while running late on the way for a training session. Poor me? Not exactly.

At the same time, there is nothing to be embarrassed about, if I can remember to say "So what?" on the days when I forget to be glad. I've been given the plenty I've been given for a reason, perhaps to grow in the gratitude that lets me freely share those riches I *should* be grateful for. It is good to be humble, but not embarrassed about by my abundance, not if I can help it. And I can.

The other day I told Lauren, who is slowly rising out of a paralyzing (and none-too-surprising) depression, that she must continue to seek out and attract people who mirror for her—who see in and reflect back to her—her greatness of spirit, passion for life and intrinsic joy. Her flat, narcissistic husband, is her mirror opposite. She tells me he lacks affect and the ability to express the kind of connection to self and others that Lauren both lives and (almost literally) is dying for.

No wonder in the mere year we've worked together as coach and client she's considered taking her life at least twice. For much of that life, she has been doing thanklessly what most would dub a "great job" of caring for others, her kids and the husband whose out-of-town job has made him as absent in body as he's long been in spirit. To a lesser extent, that's my client Liz's situation, too, her dear self buried in an overwhelming need to show up as  worthy, but rarely believing it, no matter how much good she does. There's no filling a black hole, except with light.

In *Taming The Tiger Within*, which I am still reading, Thich Nhat Hanh offers guidance Liz and Lauren, spiritual seekers both, are practicing, whether consciously or not. It is the idea that, until you make peace with your fellow human beings, you can't connect with God. "In Hanh's words, "You will not understand...the love of God, unless you practice the love of humanity."

But how on earth do you use love of humanity to bring you to God's love? That's a tall, broad order, Monsieur Monk! What does it mean and where does it leave *you* when you make caring for others your primary spiritual practice? Religious ascetics like Mother Teresa might say: *wherever you are, just show up and serve.* Give yourself over to others entirely, be it the lepers of Calcutta, the children you brought into this world, or your thirteen cats. The rest will take care of itself. But isn't that what Liz and Lauren try to do, subsume themselves in others in the name of service? I think so. It sounds good, but the problem, with them at least, is it doesn't seem to work.

Many kind, self-sacrificing women I know have ended up with no self left to sacrifice. But their *no self* is not the same "no self" spiritual seekers speak of. In the seeker's *no self* scenario, there is no self left because the seeker, presumably having focused deeply within, has burned her karma to ashes, becoming the Nobody who is Everybody, infinite as the sea and insignificant as a drop.

The no-self seeker is so aligned with Source she is free of the separative desires that define an individual self. Liz and Lauren, on the other hand, place most of their focus outside, expending themselves till the ocean is dry. Rather than burnt up and lost in the light, they get burned out and lost in the dark, till there are no resources—*no Source self*—left from which to live and give.

It apparently didn't work very well for **Mother Teresa** either. After her death and the publication of decades of personal letters to her Superiors, we learned that her self-sacrifice was neither fed by nor yielding of the divine connection she was assumed to have had and presumably yearned for. Indeed she reported regularly feeling a "deep and abiding spiritual pain," even comparing her inner experience to hell. What she herself referred to as her "hypocrisy" lasted decades, and interestingly began around the same time as she started serving the poorest lepers of Calcutta.

❧ ❧ ❧

A little later in his book, Thich Nhat Hanh inspiringly invites us to become a torch, whose flame lights others' torches. "Practicing like that," he tells us, "you can help peace and joy grow in the entire world." Yes, yes. I believe more firmly and humbly than ever that this is what I am doing and would encourage others who are open to encouragement to do. But we need guidance.

Exactly *how* do you become a torch, and what does it take to get and stay lit, always on fire with love? For most of us, it doesn't just happen because we say or wish it to be so. Both

Liz and Lauren have big hearts and an uncommon longing to serve the world. No one could argue with that. Lauren taught her prodigious theater skills to inner city children and Liz has developed an impassioned volunteer program to get women in need of jobs on their feet and working.

They devoted themselves to their families and their spiritual development as best they knew how. But both have become sick in body, mind and spirit for one crucial reason: they have little realistic sense of what it takes for us human beings to sustain ourselves in love, as they've tried with less and less good effect on themselves and others, to "love thy neighbor as thyself"—Jesus' version of Thich Nhat Hanh's exhortation to love humanity in God's stead. *Without the capacity to love and nurture ourselves, and thus keep our love pump primed, our love store is bound to run out.*

Before we can love others as God, we must learn to love *ourselves* as God, or as the decent people we are, at the least. Where else would charity begin and love originate but at home in our own dear hearts? *We cannot give what we do not have.* Lauren knows it but she hasn't lived it.

We must be full of love if we are to share love. Love must be our heartfelt experience, so alive in us that we can't help but be its first and last beneficiaries. We may be able to *act* as if we love others without loving ourselves, and that's not a bad practice if it's not mere pretense or at our own expense (as with my two clients). But until our hearts overflow with a love that knows no bounds and includes ourselves as well as the rest, we cannot love another *truly* for long.

What a conundrum! Loving ourselves, I have noticed during my thirty-year odyssey, is the hardest thing for most of us to

Loving ourselves is the hardest thing for most of us to do.

do. It is almost impossible to see ourselves clearly enough to love what we see and to treat ourselves as kindly as we deserve, unless…we have expert help.

Who would our love experts be? Anyone and everyone we can turn up in our lives who love themselves more than we love ourselves. To develop in self-love, we are wise to hang out with people having a better sense of *I* than we have—and a better *eye*, for our and their own divine nature. We must surround ourselves with those who see and love us, yes; but we will benefit especially from being with those committed to loving themselves. And they aren't hard to spot, being more than usually self-fulfilled, lively and engaging. You'll *want* to spend time with them.

Self-love, like self-hatred, is catching. Call it the *love bug*. When I am able to love my clients who are lacking in self-love, of course my love for them helps them feel more lovable. But the love I have for myself probably impacts them most. That's because we can transmit our love best through our very being, as happened to me in Bapuji's presence, via a kind of energetic osmosis. It's a great looping system, where those with less self-love get to catch the bug, while those who already love themselves get to boost their capacity to share it, as Thich Nhat Hanh suggests we do.

Indeed we can't grow in love unless and until we share it. Like water filling and spilling from a fountain, we can keep taking in more love only if we keep giving away the love we are getting. And, a critical point for me, if we are to grow in love and appreciation—for ourselves, each other and God—*we must hold that as our primary purpose and make time to practice self-love.*

> *We can't grow in love unless and until we share it.*

Wherever we are, whatever we are doing, we can seize the moment to stop, relax, feel and appreciate our holy human magnificence. In this way, we can replenish the love store, adding to our own supply, that we may hold the torch for others in a healthy, all-nourishing way. To learn to light others' flames without extinguishing our own—let alone while spurring ours to burn brighter— is the work of a lifetime, the practice of all practices. *We cannot give what we do not have.* To fully show you your magnificence—to *love* you—I have to own my magnificence and love myself. I must recognize and be grateful for all that I am and have. Only then will my light burn bright enough for me to *bring peace and joy to the entire world,* as our heart of hearts wants to do and indeed we must do if we're to survive, not only as individuals but also as a people.

In the thirty years since Lucy's death helped me come to life, I have moved in that direction at what has seemed at times a snail's pace. But moved I have, from something akin to self-hatred—a distasteful, distrustful ignorance of who I was—to something closer to self-love. It is a love that feels almost universal in its embrace, not limited to me alone. For to love ourselves completely is to love the world, and vice versa, though I am pretty sure the loving ourselves part must come first!

I sit in that love now, my heart filling my chest, providing a kind of anesthetic for my physical aches and pains. *So what if I hurt?* I am here *in love* for the moment, and what on earth is better or more important than that? But most heartening to me about this morning is how easily I sank into writing—a lot of it too—and how down and grounded I feel in my body, even as I write words about uplifting myself and others to a realm beyond the physical.

The skin and bones of me, my five senses, all of me is vividly present in this room. I gaze toward the lit Christmas tree and its lovely ornaments, each one more *there* in its place on its branch than I have ever seen it before. The twelfth day of Christmas has come and long gone, and still I want the tree up, lit and decorated, a beacon against the dreary mid-winter days. The lit tree stands too as a celebration of the new year and the light I want it to bring— for me, Trond, our children, my clients, our extended family and the entire suffering world.

As ignorance and fear threaten to destroy us in the human forms we are used to taking, we must keep fueling our torches with love, the only antidote I know to darkness and pain. *Only* love relieves suffering. So let us begin at the beginning, with love for the self. A few minutes ago as I was writing the words about my torch burning brightly, the ever-elusive January 2005 winter sun burst forth from its wintery cloud cover for a moment, before retreating again from view.

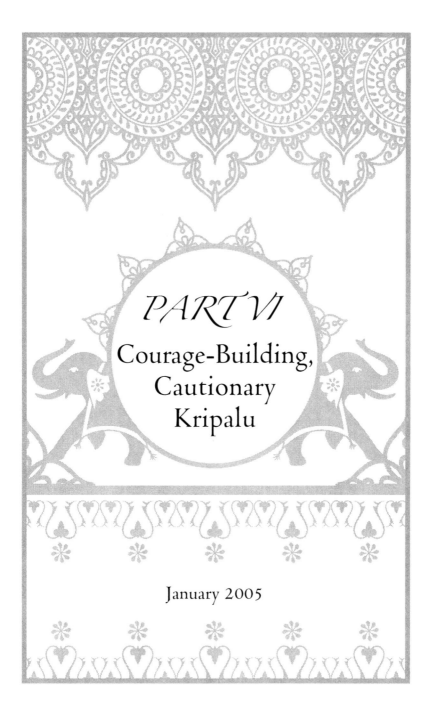

PART VI
Courage-Building, Cautionary Kripalu

January 2005

January 11, 2005

Killer Kripalu Days

Good morning! It is already 10 a.m. and gray as usual so far this year. Also just as usual, I am writing on my cozy corner of the couch, with Umesh (whose new Indian name has survived longer than Arba-Bhagul's). As he nestles beside me, a lively fire and my Christmas tree cheer me on. Trond says we must take it down on Thursday, the twentieth day of Christmas.

Meanwhile, when sister sun made a rare appearance yesterday, she showed her fiery face just long enough to call me out to trek around Silver Lake in her honor. Thanks to my murderously sore *skewed foot* (*skewed* is the term the foot doctor used to describe my two too-close-together toe bones!), it was a duty walk every step of the way. But—and it's a big but—at the other end of this decrepit body, my yearlong stiff neck, which last fall was worse than ever, may be easing up. Hallelujah.

I don't know which of the many good things I am doing for myself may be responsible: Maurie's massages, Rory's almost imperceptible tweaks, or my physical therapist Paula's strange exercises. In the oddest of these, which I also do at home, I don a thin rubber glove like a dental assistant. Then I hold my temples tight to secure my head with one hand and grip the upper jaw by the front teeth with the other, while trying to pull my top jaw over and down to the right—*hard*. Who knew? Without a better idea, I go ahead and do what I am told.

157

My strength training and regular walking may also have had a hand in my neck being better, and the nine hours of sleep I get must be helping. Even the regularity of this writing and the sense of greater usefulness it provides me could aid in my healing. God only knows how my neck got so seriously out of whack in the first place, so God alone may know what it will take for it to heal.

As part of my healing effort, I am bravely choosing to return—after a ten-year hiatus—to my longtime spiritual home, Kripalu. The program that calls me back is Panchakarma, the in-depth Indian Ayurvedic cleansing program I've done a few times elsewhere and loved. The minute I read about it in the new Kripalu program guide, I was smitten and decided I had to go.

Now, having considered the considerable cost and long drive by myself in the dead of winter, I am having second thoughts. But is it really the money—and the threat of running into a blizzard alone, as I have more than once, northeast of Scranton—that stops me? Or am I tripped up about this trip by the prospect of perhaps being made utterly vulnerable again?

Some of my life's most harrowing moments have hit within Shadowbrook's walls. There, and at the earlier Pennsylvania Kripalu ashrams during nearly

> **Shadowbrook** is the name of the facility to which Amrit Desai (whom I used to call Gurudev) moved with his Kripalu community in the mid-1980s. Situated on a huge hill overlooking a lake in Lenox, Massachusetts, the 400-acre property had been reconstituted as a Jesuit monastery after the original mansion built by Andrew Carnegie burned down. Later for many years, it housed Kripalu residents as well as guests, and to this day it is home to the ever-popular Kripalu Center.
>
> ❧ ❧ ❧

twenty years as a Kripalu disciple, teacher and leader, I
fell apart and broke open over and over again. I fell apart
physically, once for weeks as sick as I've ever been, except
when I had dysentery in India. And I fell apart mentally,
almost every time I went, my ego pummeled by two
conflicting pulls: the desire to be seen and loved, and the
dread that if I were seen, rather than being loved I'd be
exposed for the fraud I feared I was.

To my credit I kept stepping up to the plate. And I kept
getting slapped down—by the myriad mirrors offered by my
guru and his disciples—for not being fully myself. Layer by
layer, one week or weekend at a time, Kripalu dismantled
me, years before Ilana Rubenfeld and her training stripped
me bare. Hard as it was to be there, I went because Kripalu
was where I learned to love and be loved and felt more
rarely alive and capable of joy than anywhere else but India.
With each ego jolt delivered by what we called the "Kripalu
experience," I was forced further out of my bedeviled head
and down into the heart and soul of me, where love—and
I—truly live.

It was sheer torture to have my *cover* blown, or in
danger of being, by people like Taponidhi and Vasudev,
whose respect my ego lived and (with their considerable
help) ultimately died for. How badly I wanted those senior
Kripalu disciples, my teachers and mentors, to love and
value me. How terrified I was that they wouldn't, if they got
to see who this would-be yogini really was.

It's funny when I think about it. I had little sense myself
of who we would find deep down past years of deceptive
self-protective facades. But short of actual data, I must have
been proceeding on the assumption it wouldn't be pretty, or
I wouldn't have been so frightened of showing up. But show

up I did for years and years, often taking my yoga students along to watch the slaughter. For my last (now long-ago) decade there, I even put myself in the visible, ego-dicey position of a Kripalu Network Regional Leader.

Fortunately, the leadership role entailed training in spiritual mentoring skills. The combination of challenge and support slowly stripped me of the shameful false behaviors I'd long hidden behind. *I simply couldn't get away with them.* The end result of those last several years at Kripalu was to uncover for me, and for those around me, what I (and we all) are made of when we let ego go.

It turned out to be love, of course. But it sure didn't feel that way during sleepless nights in cell-like rooms once peopled by Catholic monks. How I tossed and turned. Many nights, I traipsed down long hallways to a common bathroom in hopes of relieving my near-chronic Kripalu double-whammy irritable bowel *and* bladder syndromes. My poor body was reflecting as best it could how scared shitless I was that the other Kripalu Network leaders and senior disciples I needed to like me—in order

> **The Kripalu Network** was a loose organization of Kripalu Yoga teachers and students around the country and eventually the world, as well as people who had been to Kripalu programs and wanted to keep up their yoga-related practices at home. Other Kripalu teachers and I began forming Kripalu support groups in the 1970s, and as the work spread and more groups were formed, they were clustered into regions, a leader appointed to head each one. I served as the first Mid-Atlantic Regional Leader, mentoring two dozen support group leaders in five states. I was particularly intimidated about supervising a New Jersey group leader—a male psychiatrist.
>
> ❧ ❧ ❧

for *me* to like me—would find me as full of shit figuratively as I was literally.

It is hard to remember now how much of my power I regularly gave away to other people. At the start of my Kripalu run, almost anyone anywhere could hurt me or help me feel better about myself, depending. I didn't yet know how to tend to myself, or who the self needing tending was. I craved peer attention so badly that I let it, or its more fateful *lack*, define me. What is now a mere tendency to be affected by others' opinion of me was then almost the only way I knew how to be.

When somebody liked me, I was okay, which pleased me for the moment. If someone didn't like me, or I thought they didn't, *there was something wrong with me*. If that person mattered to me, I felt unlovable and miserable, for much longer than I'd been happy when I thought I was liked. It took a lot of those shakedown (by shaking me up) roller-coaster rides to realize nothing was ever wrong with me—except that I was foolish enough to think so and act as if I had something to hide.

What needed stripping away in the name of freedom was not the real me at all, of course, but the false "cover" self (or *selves*)—the pretense created in ignorance and long shored up by shame and fear. And stripped near-naked I'd eventually be, at risk of frostbite from a less than warm reception by anyone who might see and not adore *the real me* (and there would be those). But first the pain of keeping up the sham that all was well—and I was cucumber cool in there behind my many masks—had to grow greater than the fear of being rejected as unworthy of being seen.

A day came when I reached a critical tipping point, one fear overtaking the other, forcing the strip-down. I say the tipping point was *critical* because the ego-wrenching transformation I endured is not something we usually choose to undertake—unless and until the sting of staying the same and holding down the old fort threatens to overwhelm us and take us down. Why would we invite the horrific psychic pain of exposing our presumed-to-be *fearsome* authentic self if we didn't have to? Most of us need to get darned dissatisfied with our stinky status quo before we'll want to rock the boat—even if it won't sink *us* but only drown the persona we've pretended and tried hard to be.

My tipping point came during a workshop where our stalwart Network leader Vasudev overtly called my bluff on an inauthentic thing I said to a group of peers. I can't remember the details but I sure remember the effect— and my affect. I fell into a shame as profound as I ever remember feeling. I was more mortified than the time I was caught gleefully playing with myself under the desk in first grade and my parents were brought in to deal with their sexually precocious little girl.

Being so young, I may have gotten over that one in a hurry (or maybe not). But I burned for weeks in the shame of Vasudev's public unmasking, until it all but burned the old me up. From then on I figured it would be easier to try to play it straight and take my chances. For me, shame beats all other dreaded emotions hands-down—and what a bummer, since facing and erasing our shame is what it often takes to let go of the selves we've contrived, so as to become the self that we are.

So yes, I am pretty darned sure I hesitate to revisit Kripalu now for the same reason I hesitated to visit it way back when: for fear of stirring the waters of my self—and self-image—once more. I know as well as my English and Sanskrit names that the churning and burning likely to result from showing up there again may blow me—and whatever may remain of my old carefully-contrived covers—right out of the water and into the fire of transformation. Shit.

Though it may well be time for a new round in the battle with ego, it is one excruciating proposition.

> **Sanskrit names** are given to disciples on the Kripalu Yoga path. When I was initiated in 1972, I was given the name Bakula, which Gurudev told me means "the guru's scent."
>
> ❖ ❖ ❖

Facing ourselves full-on requires immense courage, and I honestly wonder if I've got the heart and guts it takes right now. What a great day it will be when I—and for that matter, all of us—can look forward to and welcome such radical shape-shifting transformation. Till then, I suppose the brave among us will feel the fear and do it anyway. May God bless us on our way!

January 12, 2005

Leaving Kripalu Behind

This Wednesday morning may be the grayest day of the
year yet, which is saying something, given the winter
we've been having. Yesterday, after a teasing snowflake or
two mid-morning, it rained cats and dogs all day. Almost
two weeks into this new year and not one whole sunny
day or decent snowfall to spell the torrents. A Central
Pennsylvania record must be going down.

But we know it's perfect, if not fun, for me to be left
alone in the gloom. With Trond gone east to Lebanon for
a meeting, and all gray and quiet on the western front, I
am practically forced to sit here and write. How could I *not*
when my life conspires to make it this easy? Nora's lemon
butter Christmas cookies, which I've been nibbling on—
just one each morning for the past two weeks (now that's
discipline!)—are still in evidence (yum, yum). And although
the tree comes down tomorrow (boo hoo), it's still up today,
lighting *me* up as we speak (yay). Things could be worse.

Cookies, tree or no, I always have the cozy fire Trond
makes me, and surely more quiet days to come, urging me
inward as they do, to write my way toward the light. Many
authors, I gather, compose from suffering, to alleviate a
psychic itch they can't quite reach. But remembering Maha's
question about whether I am ready to grow without pain, I
wonder if I am learning to *write* without pain, sometimes
even from a place of joy or at least of relative peace. Let's see.

To begin preparing myself for even the idea of a return
trip to Kripalu, I've done something else in addition to

yesterday's intense writing jag about my Kripalu past. I went through the Kripalu curriculum guide, forcing myself to read program descriptions and study the faces of teachers I knew who are still involved there today. Seeing them on the page made me so queasy I shut the quarterly booklet and stuffed it away. I resent having felt I had to fly from the nest on my own while others were content to stay. And I'm jealous of the few I know have less to offer than I do but lead programs there while I sit home in obscurity. It was a hard heart (and ego) break.

In May 1994 at a large Kripalu Network gathering in Rhode Island, I made my farewell in a thankful, tearful talk to the dear men and women I'd worked and played with for almost twenty years. I left because I knew with a deep-down, true-as-can-be knowing that much as I hated to lose good friends, I was done there—the guru and his retinue having had their (spiritual) way with me.

I had met myself, and my brothers and sisters—as we called each other—head-on, in fear and in love. Realizing at last what we humans are made of, I was ready to see what *I* could make of that bittersweet knowledge out beyond Kripalu's once protective but finally constraining walls.

Well before I left, I had begun to see and despair of the guru's failings; how he seemed stuck in a self-absorbed, self-satisfied (really *dissatisfied*) rut he wasn't willing to see. I remember standing wistfully in the back of the room my last time at Kripalu. Gurudev was perfunctorily performing his saffron-robed role, inviting and responding to the same old disciples' same old questions.

As often before, a physician who, like me, had spent nearly twenty years at the guru's feet, asked yet another "relationship" question. I watched Gurudev answer glibly, dispensing gratuitous advice from high on his velvet throne. The doctor was an accomplished grown man. He should long since have been lifted up off the floor and urged to find answers within. I left the room, the sick feeling in my stomach yet another confirmation that the time had come for me to move on.

Then, and in the months leading up to that last sad day, I saw the guru not practicing what he preached, what I'd learned from him and the disciples he had trained and who had trained me. In a memorable talk years before, Gurudev had told us about the "pathless path" and the need he'd felt to take off from the prescribed way—to carve out a path of his own. He seemed to imply that just as he'd had to differentiate himself from Bapuji, we too would one day need to leave him behind.

He must have known then what I now understand: that if we follow another's path for too long, it becomes our religion, rife with dogma that destroys the soul. He must have known and forgotten. Great teachers train students by encouraging them to take risks, spread their wings and fly. After all, that is what Bapuji had done when he sent Amrit off, at the age of seventeen, to teach in America.

Probably sensing he was about to lose even the semblance of power, Gurudev clung to what was left of his by clinging to—rather than empowering—us, his spiritual children. The tighter his grip, the weaker he got. At last he appeared to me to be defensive, bored and boring, inadvertently pushing me (and others) from the nest. I later realized his behavior must have turned narcissistic, a danger for charismatic leaders— and a cautionary tale for the natural-born teacher I am.

January 13, 2005

My Guru's Nasty Fall

I feel very lucky to have come and gone from Kripalu, and to have embraced and released the priceless guru experience exactly when I did. Less than six months after saying my farewells, Gurudev was thrown from his throne in a nasty sex scandal. My once yoga student, longtime Kripalu resident and always friend Dennis, called from Shadowbrook to tell me on the day the ugly news broke. "Are you sitting down?" he asked, and somehow I knew what was coming.

I was interested in a prurient sort of way. But I was neither shocked nor disappointed. I knew by then Gurudev was no longer who he pretended and surely wanted to be. His sacred yogic teachings were bound to be purer than the real human being conveying them. I wasn't surprised they took firmer hold in me, Dennis and other dedicated students than they had in him. While he was busy performing—and sadly exploiting—his guru role, we were gladly exploring our hearts. While he got caught up in being the messenger, we ran to our practice mats to get the message.

One message *I* got is that human beings have secret shadow sides we had better get in touch with and pay attention to. I learned that from practicing his Kripalu Yoga, which I did as a sort of self-therapy, having discovered that yoga breathing and postures could put me in touch with—and help me release—old unexpressed feelings lodged in my body and blocking my throat and heart.

Using yoga to bring dark unconscious parts of myself into the light of awareness, so they could be expressed and integrated or released, became a regular part of my practice. (This was before the formal Yoga Therapy system pioneered by a Kripalu student and teacher, Michael Lee.) But Gurudev, being an Indian man of humble origins, not a psychologically savvy American like Lee and me—and an isolated guru to boot—apparently missed all that and mismanaged his shadow side. He was all tied up trying to look and act as good as he thought a guru should—like Bapuji.

So Gurudev must not have known that our shadows grow in proportion to our attempts to ignore them and act better than we are. In order to dissipate, shadows need exposure to the light of consciousness and our own compassion. They thrive and get the better of us when they are given the short shrift he likely gave his. It is perhaps understandable that he didn't know what the hell to do with the likes of his lust, though he no doubt knew that what he did do with it was wrong, especially since he continued insisting his unmarried resident disciples practice *Brahmacharya*.

> **Brahmacharya** means conduct that leads to the realization of Brahman or one's Higher Self, including study of the Vedic Scriptures. In American yoga parlance, though, it often refers mainly to self-restraint and mastery of sexual and carnal desire in thought, word and deed, i.e., no sex.
>
> ❖ ❖ ❖

Bapuji may have handled his dark side by staying so much out of the world and its temptations, contemplating his demons right along with his God. Who knows? Gurudev, we know, was very much *in* the world, letting at

least some of his demons run him. He paid the price for
not working out (or airing out) his fantasies by *acting* them
out, being found out and having his dirty laundry publicly
aired. Behind his perfect guru facade was a man with needs
and—his feet kissed too many times perhaps—a growing
hubris bound to bring him down. It doesn't excuse, but may
explain his sordid personal behavior and its stark contrast
to the benign public persona and work.

Amrit, as we quickly began to call him, crashed and
burned—and was soon forced out—amidst mounting
accusations of his cavalier sexual exploits, by disciples
young enough to be his daughters. We learned he'd also
had a long adulterous affair with his closest associate, the
ashram's senior administrator, who at least was closer
in age. The young ones must have worshipped him as a
Demigod, a point he'd apparently played upon to garner
their sexual favors. It was very ugly, especially for those
who'd moved to Kripalu and dedicated their lives to its
success. Many disciples understandably threw the baby out
with the bathwater and wanted none of it. But for me the
message Amrit Desai delivered, which I took in over two
decades and which transformed me totally, was unsullied by
revelations of his seamy, steamy exploits.

If I entertained the idea of Amrit Desai as a near God,
or godlier than I am—and I *must* have early on—that
illusion was long gone by 1994, the year I left (in May)
and he fell (in October). Thanks to his potent ancient
teachings and my God-given capacity to integrate them
into a contemporary woman's life, I had embarked on the
disengagement process years before I up and flew the coop.

Along with the graceful yoga he taught me, I am forever
indebted to Amrit Desai, for showing me, through the

effects of his *not* doing it, the immense value—for teacher as well as student—of stepping down and back from the limelight whenever we possibly can. I am grateful to have learned in such a clear and graphic way that the job of a spiritual teacher is nothing more or less than to cheer people on to limelights of their own. He didn't do that and got burned out and up.

January 14, 2005

Stepping Back from the Light

Years before my guru days, as a young blazing Leo, I had begun a process of stepping into—then back from—the limelight, through the medium of theater. My childhood passion for acting was generously fueled by our live-in Aunt Del, whose husband had been a Hollywood voice coach. Recognizing my thespian penchant, Del had a stage built in our basement, where she directed plays starring me and the neighbor kids. I went on to do summer theater and was thrilled when, in Seattle at nineteen, I landed the lead role in the American premiere of a small play by Harold Pinter. I was center stage with almost all the lines at a theater-in-the-round. Talk about the limelight!

But not for long. Back in New York that fall and the next summer, the theater director at my college had it out for me, and in for another actress he'd been grooming for all the good parts long before I came on the scene. He cut me out and her *in* to every good part I was right for. I got disappointed but I didn't get the message. It took a gruesome death for me to understand that theater was not to be my path, and the public eye a dangerous place for some of us to play, at least until we've done the private dirty work that breeds humility, self-understanding and self-respect.

The casualty of my lose-the-limelight wake-up call was a writer named Richard whose highly personal Holocaust play I was directing in Philadelphia, where I lived and worked post-college. Soon after we'd cast a talented actor to play the part of the author (but thinly disguised) and started rehearsals, Richard went stark raving mad. He kidnapped his young daughter for a cross-country road trip during which he had a stroke that left him wordless. Back home and no longer able to read or write, Richard hung himself in his closet, and the spotlight lost its luster for me.

I used to say I gave up the theater. But I now realize it was the other way around. The universe used my last least glorious dramatic foray to send me the clearest possible signal to get and stay off the stage. I haven't written, directed or acted in another play since. Chances are I never will.

But it was not till ten years later, through the practice and teaching of Kripalu Yoga that I began to understand how absolutely critical and useful it was for me to step back from any stage and let others shine. I, who like the charismatic guru had tendencies to be the star—a would-be Icarus setting out for the sun only to crash and burn in the form of an author-effigy—needed to learn to become the moon. If I was not to burn up or out as I went forth in the world, I'd have to learn to pass off my sizzling Leo brilliance to those whose dimmer lights wanted extra illumination.

I would have to temper my radiance, which was too unbridled to be of utmost use to me or anyone else, while inviting others to bask in it till they too were lit up from within. It's akin to what Thich Nhat Hanh said about allowing ourselves to be a torch whose flame lights other torches. To keep my fiery ego out of it, I would need to find ways to act from behind the scenes, becoming the metaphorical life of the party whose name and face no one can later quite recall.

To become the pale moon and reflect others' light was the succinct assignment given me during a reading by an astrologer yoga student of mine. It's what I began learning to do at Kripalu: to burn off as much of me that was not true, humble and clear as I could—so I might mix up the rest with what I was learning from yoga and use it to kick-start the soul work of others.

Dear Kathy, for years my closest yoga student, and the one above all who taught me to step back and lend my light to another's torch, a few months ago wrote to acknowledge a capacity she had recognized in me before—to *ignite souls*, as I think she put it. Kathy was prompted by a poetry book she'd received, *Prayers to the Infinite*, written by another of my students, Danna Faulds.

Kathy wrote: "Your name in (Danna's) dedication so sweetly and simply tells the story of the immeasurable impact you have had on the lives of so many people— people that you have steered onto the just right path at the just right time. As you know, I am one of those people. Carolyn Myss speaks of people that we have soul contracts with…people we were destined to meet in this lifetime. I sense that your soul does its work by being in the right place at the right time to meet a great many souls…and in that way you are an awakener."

I am incredibly touched by Kathy's words, which feel true to me at the level of heart. It *is* my job to light souls. I am here to bring people to the spiritual table, not to feed them, but to teach them to feed themselves—*with themselves*—through self-love, that most fortifying food for the soul.

> *A speck of dust from the guru's feet*
> *Forms a bridge strong enough to cross.*
> *Samskara will be overcome.*
> *Worship him as the lord of all.*

> **Samskara** has many meanings. But here it seems to refer to the accumulated impressions made upon our beings through our thoughts, words and deeds. It is related to what we call our *karma*.
>
> ❖ ❖ ❖

Though I love that verse from the *Sri Guru Gita*, which comes to mind on reading Kathy's words, *I would not be a guru*. Never. No disciples bowing to kiss my holy lotus feet, thank you very much. I would be—indeed I am—a sister seeker at the table of spiritual crumbs, who when we get lucky—and graceful—enough, may feast with my tablemates on whole cakes and sweet icing too! A spiritual teacher does not a *guru* need to be.

The path of a guru can be a lonely one. Increasingly lost and isolated in his insular world, mine seemed inept at intimate human interaction, the give and take it takes to light us up on the worldly plane. I could see it in his ever more empty eyes. Ironically, it was Bapuji, who lived alone in silence for years—rarely surrounded by family and disciples as Gurudev was—who had the innate capacity to connect. I could see it in his sparkling eyes. He looked anything but lonely, presumably because through his relentless self-scrutiny he knew in his bones and nerves, as well as with his bright mind, the thing he often told us, that "the whole world is one family."

I too am coming to know in my bones something of what he must have meant. I feel less separate from others than ever before. That's because, as Bapuji must have done, I am getting more in touch with and easy about the whole of me, shadow side as well as light. It's only now as I am more connected to all of myself, and so to others, that I realize how terribly separate I used to be.

I wasn't any more separate then than I am now, of course. But I felt that way, off spinning in my own little space capsule, not as different from Gurudev as I may first have imagined. I too could be self-absorbed and disconnected, watching what I said and did from behind my many roles. How hard I tried to keep others from bumping against me, knocking me over or out of the game, or I them. And that self-conscious caution kept me from getting close enough to bump into people to *good* effect either. It was a rare person, like Trond, with whom I dared share a lot of myself.

Given all that concern about getting judged and hurt—*about whether I was good enough*—no wonder I woke up nervous on days when I had a yoga class to teach, especially in the early years. Even recently as a new life coach, I could be nervous picking up the phone to support a client. When we separate ourselves from others in fear, we put ourselves on the firing line. We stand before the judge, awaiting the incoming outside verdict, about us and our every move. We play it small, safe, in the box. Hawk-like, we watch others watch us and can easily feel we come up short.

When we separate ourselves from others in fear, we put ourselves on the firing line.

It is probably the fear of coming up short that kept me from Kripalu these ten years since I (and the guru) left. I was afraid I might not measure up—in my own eyes and the eyes of some who stayed. But you know what? It's okay to have stayed away, even if it was partly shame that kept me. After years of blood, sweat and teary personal growth work, it was time to make and take a break. I was ripe and ready for the "retreat from battle" sanctioned by Bapuji in my favorite Bapuji talk about the humanity of struggle. I had to cut the umbilical cord to keep on growing *me*.

I am a strange bird, if not as fiercely independent as Trond. Of course I had to strike out on my own to uncover and fully express all of who I am. The next stage of my search called for fewer familiar *reflections* and more unfamiliar *reflection*, an inner engagement to gauge myself and my progress in contexts of my own making. To *come into my own* and know the whole world

Of course I had to strike out on my own to uncover and fully express all of who I am.

as one family, like Bapuji, I had to relinquish the insular path—and its pack—to pursue a wider pathless path. A return to Kripalu may be as good an indicator as any of how well I have fared by myself.

PART VII
A Confidence
Born of
Self-Care

January 2005

January 15, 2005

Holiday Victories and
a Book in the Works

Yesterday's call with Maha, back from a holiday visit with family in Paris, went for a generous hour, not the stringent forty-five minutes she used to hold to tightly as a second skin. I love her new ease and generosity of spirit and the increased freedom it speaks of and promises, for her and for me. I started our call by telling her about what I see as the two greatest successes of my holidays.

The first is how well I've honored myself and my path, which seems particularly consequential given what I could have viewed and treated as significant family demands. During the entire two weeks Teg, Heather and Jasper were visiting us over Christmas, I did what I needed to do for me before all else. I didn't let guilt or codependence drive me. And thanks to a strong commitment to my own self-care, I was more graciously and gladly able to do what was needed for others as well.

Weekday mornings after Trond left for Lebanon, for example, I stayed upstairs till I was good and ready to come down. Hearing Jasper and one or the other of his doting parents up and about with him in the kitchen, I took my time instead of rushing to be with them. Having rested and cared for myself first, I could pitch in from a place of ease and joy. Caring for my first grand boy was a delight when, rather than imposing it, I chose it from a place of self-compassion and respect.

After one of the several nights when Jasper woke up crying in the unfamiliar crib that was once his daddy's, I sent his exhausted parents back to bed. Although I had work to do, I spirited the little guy away to my office, where we hung out like the co-conspirators we aren't yet but may soon become. While I wrote emails, he played happily on the floor with my big pink and lime plastic paper clips and the other meager toy-like pickings I found among my office detritus.

After a while, he approached my chair and lifted his tiny arms high into the air, which I took to mean he wanted to join me. Onto my lap he came, where he sat still as a little angel. I held his warm baby body close to mine while I continued working at my computer. We swayed together to the Christmas music in the background till Jasper fell sound asleep in my arms.

Trond and I carried him to a couch in the guest room near my office. There, wrapping Christmas presents, we kept our eye on him, as he and his parents slept on. My heart swells even now as I remember our tender time together—a rare experience, Teg told me, for the usually super-active fourteen-month-old. The more I nurture myself and do only what I love, the sweeter life gets.

My other holiday success—a greater self-confidence and sense of well-being, and so enjoyment of life itself—is related to the first one. The more I treat myself as if I am worth it, the more worthy I see that I am. The growing self-worth encourages me to keep up the self-care, which in turn lets me feel and act my best, bringing out the best in others too, a healthy recipe for thriving.

The more I treat myself as if I am worth it, the more worthy I see that I am.

This greater confidence born of self-care that I'm feeling must be why, day after day, I dare sit here with pen to page, trusting that although I don't yet know where it's going, I am doing what I'm meant to do. I am letting my heart drive my head and my hand, as I record what swells up from my depths to be recognized. I am writing in this newly surrendered, organic way to uncover what I know—what we all know but may need to be reminded of—about who we are and how we can reclaim that glorious essential self of ours, for our good and the good of all.

I am writing in this newly surrendered, organic way to uncover what I know — what we all know but may need to be reminded of — about who we are and how we can reclaim that glorious essential self of ours, for our good and the good of all.

Never before have I known such a steady true collaboration between my head and my heart. The wordsmith between my ears is finally in service not to the ego and some elusive dream of a book-to-be, but to my very soul, and so by extension to yours. I write my particular story as it unfolds, uncovering and discovering myself and yourself, our fundamental common self, from the inside out, one sentence, phrase, and sometimes word at a time. It is a remarkable experience.

If this is to be a book, it will not be a memoir written after the fact about some done-deal transformation, or like Tolle's work, an impersonal view from already enlightened heights. This writing itself is part of our transformation, you looking over my shoulder with me as *we* struggle in real time to be free. My struggle is your struggle, the unfolding of my evolution so raw, real and immediate it touches into the universal core we share. Arising from the essential experience of one awakening soul, these words speak to many souls—because we are one soul, together *in spiritus.*

I mean to offer here everything that I have, know and am, whatever might uplift us from our mortal suffering into the sure knowledge we are worthy exactly the way we are, and that we and our God are one. Why shouldn't *I*, who am ordinary in so many ways, do this one extraordinary thing? Why not I, who have been beyond blessed with God-given gifts, great teachers, and decades dedicated to self-observation, writing and service, yet who am not so different from you?

Why shouldn't I, who am ordinary in so many ways, do this one extraordinary thing?

Indeed I *must* do this thing, must take the trouble— if it is trouble—to keep writing, and to call to myself the resources that can help me turn it all—poems, stories, and especially these journal entries—into a book worthy of the abundance I have been given to share. Yesterday, Maha asked me to write more about my writing, to let this very process help me uncover and face my fear of it, and perhaps to understand the need I have felt recently for a writing partner to bolster me up.

Even as Maha and I spoke, I began to realize that much as I may think I want a collaborator, this writing project is mine alone to do. No one else can write this. Rather than a coauthor, what I may need is a loving agent or editor who understands me and what I am doing. Maha told me yesterday that while in France, she finished *her* book, just as she—ambitious lady—had planned. An editor with a small publishing house is helping her, she said, as she moves toward printing the book.

Maha offered to tell her publisher about me. I am encouraged and hopeful I may finally be ready to "bite the bullet," as I put it to Maha yesterday, and do this book thing that till now has seemed hard as steel. I'm not the only one who needs to be ready, of course. The universe, co-conspirator in all things creative and fun, must also be prepared to play. Perhaps it is, and I am too. We'll see.

January 17, 2005

The Importance of Being Suzanne

I t's a strange morning in which I am unexpectedly finding time to write. Last night the worldly woman and little girl in me were both delighted to discover the Golden Globe Awards on TV. I loved every minute of the surprisingly moving show. I find movie stars entrancing to watch, as stars of all stripes should be. In accepting their awards, some of the honorees were overcome with warm, transparent gratitude for being recognized, which made them human and easy to relate to. As reality TV goes, awards shows are the best, full of those shining stars, showing up in real (if too late) time. Having stayed awake watching past 11, I slept badly for the third night in a row.

Not a good thing, that! Fuel for body and soul is more critical than ever now that the weather has changed, from mild but gray, to bright and bitterly cold. It was down to 10 degrees Fahrenheit last night. The snow that blanketed us the night before last shimmers bright white through the few windowpanes Jack Frost forgot to etch with icing. I'm bundled up tight but sneezing even so, as I try to revive two dying fires, one across the room, and the other inside my skin.

The logs in our usually trusty little fireplace are wet and smoking, with no flames in sight. They will ignite in time. I'm more concerned about the dying inner fire. My passion for a book got doused yesterday by the cold water of what two bright, enthusiastic book coaches told me it takes to make a book happen. It was the same sorry story I got ten years ago. My problem, I struggled to explain to the two women, whom I spoke with by phone, is that I don't want to *make it happen.*

I don't want to do what I don't want to do, my familiar litany. And it was pretty easy to tell from how yucky I felt part way through our long-awaited call that I don't want to do most of what these

I don't want to do what I don't want to do, my familiar litany.

women, like Meredith, Toni and others before and after, believe I will have to do to produce and publish a book. It all sounds hard, unpleasant, and at the risk of sounding naive, unnecessary.

I don't, for instance, want to research the self-help market so as to *strategically position* my book based on how similar to or different it is from other books that sell well—*the successful competition.* I don't want to read or even skim those other books, as the book coaches say I must. And though I enjoyed preparing a book proposal years ago, I don't want to write one this time, or to answer the *five critical questions* these women believe all authors must address before they *query agents,* something we know I've done before and definitely don't want to do again. It couldn't be clearer.

The women I spoke with allowed that self-publishing is an option. But recalling how my friend Jackie filled orders for her first self-published book one at a time, I find that idea less appealing and maybe more appalling than trying to land a publisher. As for getting people to buy the book, both Jackie and Meredith (who has an agent and is multi-published with a big house) say they have to do their own marketing—and you know we aren't talking about grocery shopping here.

These dedicated authors have had to place ads,

call bookstores, set up signings, write articles and, as
Meredith recently told me about her latest book, scramble
for every last shred of publicity they receive. It's not that I
can't do those things. I am uncommonly good at them, or
used to be. It's that my whole being is reviled by the mere
mention of doing any, let alone *all* of that. But why? Am
I afraid, as Maha seems to suspect? Or am I being lazy, or
stubbornly anti-authoritarian, the unruly Rebel she has
identified in me, unwilling to play the game by others'
"stupid" rules?

I *am* scared, we know. I can be lazy. And yes, I like to do
things my own peculiar way, not somebody else's. But I am
also brave, hardworking and willing to do what's necessary
to be of service to others and to the call of my own great
soul. I rarely if ever let fear stop me when something gets
my attention. My countless scary trips to Kripalu over two
decades show that. And signing up with Ilana to work my
terrified ass off trying to fit into—then shed—the teacher's
perfectionist mold, proves I can and will do almost anything
I find compelling and right for me.

Toward the end of the call with the book coaches, one
said: "You have to decide whether you want this book more
than you don't want to do the things you don't want to do."
Bingo! In other words, is a book important enough for me
to be willing to suffer the process? While I wasn't happy
about it, I was near certain from how badly I felt that no
book is worth suffering for.

I hung up disappointed, deflated and sad. But thanks
to my ever-supportive, insightful and ingenious husband,
I was not down for long. With a few thoughtful words,
he reminded me I was falling into an old, all-too-familiar
trap: thinking I need to do things just like everybody else

does (or says), and listening to *them* instead of paying attention to my usually reliable inner promptings.

I told the coaches yesterday I need the book process to be easy—simple even—and that I believe

I was falling into an old, all-too-familiar trap: thinking I need to do things just like everybody else.

it can be, though I wasn't as confident about it then as I may sound now. To their credit, they seemed open to the possibility of an easier way, and wished me success with it. They kindly asked me to stay in touch, and I just might. I like them and I love the idea of a team to support me, but their (for me too formulaic) soup-to-nuts approach to publication is probably not for me.

Meanwhile, there was Trond with a perspective that understands and appreciates who I am and directs me back to myself, my heart and my inimitable way (even when I don't yet know what it is). Trond sees and believes what I too truly believe but lose sight of: that I not only can, but I *must* share who I am and what I have to offer from my own angle, however strangely slanted.

Only then will my offering be as wholehearted, authentic and effective as I am at my best. *How* I put forth my words must reflect the same energy and integrity as the words themselves and be in alignment with them—or what am I offering *but* words? If I bend myself out of shape doing others' uncomfortable bidding to get the word out, what am I saying? That life is hard? That we must squeeze our round selves into square holes to succeed? That the means, however out of kilter with one's ends and values—and in this case, with the essence of a person's life work, the very theme of her book—justify the ends? I don't buy it, because that has not been my experience.

If I were to agree to go through what feels to me like hell in order to publish, I'd be obliterating the most essential learning of my last thirty years: that we enjoy true success only by becoming supremely aware, thoughtful and trusting of our dear selves; discovering and doing whatever it is *we* love to do; and not least, doing it *our way*. If I am to do what I'm here to do, I must walk that talk of mine, every step of the way toward talking my walk (meaning the book). To let up on living from those hard-won particular truths would be to let me, and everybody else, down.

We enjoy true success only by becoming supremely aware, thoughtful and trusting of our dear selves; discovering and doing whatever it is we love to do; and not least, doing it our way.

Trond, God bless him, really gets the importance of honoring our uniqueness. He holds that space for both of us. Maybe it's because, as he says, he's getting stranger too. He likes to tell me I only put up with him because I am as strange as he is. We talk about how different we are from almost everyone we know, two oddball peas in our pod. We are different from each other, too, of course. But we are both highly unconventional people trying to get comfy with our respective weirdnesses, in that way very much alike, and I realize, awfully good for each other.

This lovely man saved the day yesterday by suggesting for the umpteenth time that if sharing myself and what I'm learning is as important as having a book on the shelf with my name on it, there are other ways to go. If a book is too hard, I could "go virtual," creating a blog where I post my writings, or find another publication route kinder and truer to my vulnerable self. My heart quickened, and my belly, sickened by the "reality check" of the book call, calmed right down.

Isn't it great how Trond keeps in mind and oh-so-patiently repeats back what he has heard me say and seen me do, till I get the message of my own heart? Yesterday he said he saw a similarity with how I became a coach, finding ways both to deal with my fears and to get around the specified training and certification process, which seemed an unappetizing, overly systematic row to hoe at my age and stage of life. What a good parallel, and how relieved I felt after we talked about it.

As he kindly reminded me, becoming a coach my way involved committing to no more than a single introductory weekend, where my success in the practice coaching sessions emboldened me to ask a few friends to be my guinea pigs at home. It took time to gain confidence and a level of comfort with the ensuing phone sessions. But it happened. Slowly, surely, my practice grew—without my having to go to a lot of trainings in a row, jump through certification hoops, or do any heavy-duty marketing, things that many coach colleagues thought *de rigueur*. Within a year, I was sure that—dare I say it?—I was a great coach, with little left to learn from coaching trainers.

A few years into my practice, I also realized I had evolved a style of my own, including teaching, mentoring and advising my clients, which brings all of me and my life experience to bear. I knew that some of what I was doing was out of bounds vis-à-vis common coaching practice at the time. While that made me nervous, it also solidified my sense that the close supervision of certification (which several of my clients who were becoming coaches went on to do) would never feel right.

As I'd felt happening with the Rubenfeld work, even during the training, I sensed I might run into trouble being my full-blown, outrageous self within the confines of the certification process. As coaching systems go, mine was a good one. But like other models and teachers I've drawn from, notably Amrit and Ilana, I needed sooner or later to withdraw, out of what seemed a legitimate fear the system might limit me, keeping me from my self—and from *being* myself.

I notice I feel quite queasy writing about my resistance to following the crowd and fitting into the mode or mold. *Am I afraid I'll be limited?* Or, having not fit in with the stuffy homogeneous WASPs on Philadelphia's Main Line—and having felt badly for being the odd girl out—do I fear being judged again as *other*, *less than*, and *strange*? Am I scared I'll be as *ashamed* of myself as an unusual adult here, now, as I once was for being a *special* child there, then? Yes, *yes*.

My heart swells in resonance with truth, and my eyes well with tears. Little Suzie wants to avoid situations where her differences stand out. To this day, I want to fit in if I can—and *so what*? I am as human as the next girl in my desire for love and acceptance. I still want to avoid showing up and being singled out as *peculiar* (a favorite damning word of my mother's about people who appeared different from her). Phew! It can be hard not to want to join the team, run with the pack or be willing to do the deal that just about everyone says is required to do the deal. It's lonely.

But standing alone may be an act of self-salvation, a means of honoring and stoking our soul fire, that it might burn bright enough to help light a suffering world. The more we are ourselves, however wild, wired or otherwise weird, the more useful we are to everybody. Why? Because freedom and the bliss it brings come from becoming so truly who we—and *only* we—are, that we touch into the collective core. And from that universal place in us we can speak to and, in my case I also hope, *with and for* those who seek core truth themselves. We can help to heal the world.

The more we are ourselves, however wild, wired or otherwise weird, the more useful we are to everybody.

It is a demanding business becoming ourselves. As the yogic scriptures warn, we may have to leave everything behind—or at least be *willing* to. When the Gita exhorts us to *Give up even thy soul to him*, "him" refers to the external guru, of course. But more critically in the later stages of our path, the *Gita* is asking us to give our self up and over to the *inner* guru, what the *Gita* calls—and I love this—*the tiny person within the heart*. We must let go even of our idea of our self, in pursuit of naked soul truth.

More even than Trond, I must continue to trust myself and that tiny person within my heart. Being true to myself and the way that feels right to—and for—me is far more important than producing a book or sharing myself and my supposed wisdom with anyone, let alone everyone. We shall see what, if anything, I choose to do with the book coaches' guidance and the far more touching and resonant suggestions made by my blessed mirror Trond. God bless us all, as we make our way, whether alone or immersed in the lonely crowd, through the darkness that leads to its sister light.

January 19, 2005

Self-Acknowledgment Be Praised!

I t's still bitterly cold, and the promising orange glow on the eastern horizon at seven thirty this morning was quickly obscured by that ubiquitous gray sky, hinting at snow to come. My only coaching call this wintry day got canceled. Trond is out at our plant again, having decided for now that showing up there each morning at eight is his job to do. I admire his discipline and commitment. He is up at six for his daily ablutions and breakfast, before feeding and watering Nora's horse Lady Jane (the none-too-suitable name our big mare came with).

Trond hits the road by seven Monday through Friday— rain, hail, lightening, thunder, as the old football chant says, not to mention, lately, snow. I envy his sense of duty and that he feels there is somewhere he *has* to be. I don't see why he needs to go every day, and he says he doesn't want to, but still he goes. He is willing to do what he doesn't want to do. I'd rather he do what he loved. But his keeping our energy plant alive and well keeps this girl living in the manner to which she is accustomed, allowing her not to do what she doesn't want to do, and not least, to write.

I seem pretty sure about what I don't want to do, but do I know what I *do* want to do? There's no time like January 2005, with its portentous ring, to get clear as a New Year's celebration bell about why I am here. How though? Some folks I know who seem normal—or not altogether crazy anyway—say they get help with their worldly plans and pursuits from otherworldly sources like spirit guides, power animals, angels, their dead grandfather, a psychic aunt, and/ or God.

People journey with shamans, pray with priests, ask what Jesus would do and seem to get answers. An early coaching client of mine said she was inundated with heavenly guidance galore from the voices in her head. They could be so insistent she sometimes had trouble tuning them out and shutting them up. The only guidance I get from voices in my head is from those old familiar so-called tapes of conditioned beliefs I've accumulated along my way. It's a ghostly, sometimes ghastly chorus, which I've happily not altogether heeded, nor yet fully deleted. They sing on.

The closest I come to otherworldly direction is writing like this, when I can tap into a knowing greater than mind's. *So what do I want?* The answer is easy—it came right to me. *I want to be recognized widely and well for the wise and wonderful woman I am.* As those alliterative words rush my mind, I burst into sweet tears. We are not supposed to say things like that, however true they may be. It *is* true, of course, that I want to be appreciated, and as part of that, called upon to offer myself and my growing wisdom wherever in the wider world I might be of service. But it's interesting the answer that came to me said nothing about the service part, only the recognition.

The other true thing in the answer I got is harder and sweeter to say: that I am wise and—I have very mixed emotions about expressing this one on the page—*wonderful.* Yes, I may be generous, funny, smart, quirky and interesting; those I can admit to, at least sometimes. But *wonderful?* I'm weeping hard now and full of wonder about why. Could it be that *self*-acknowledgment is more essential than even the grandest outside recognition? Is seeing and appreciating myself and my substantial progress toward wholeness what I most want—maybe most *need*—in order to grow in courage and love? Might we *all* benefit from bathing like this in our wonderful selves? I think so.

As I bawl like a baby, Cider (or is he still *Umesh?*) lies purring contently beside me. Does he know, as his odd little smile suggests, that these are tears of gratitude and joy, and not as sometimes, of psychic pain? Oh, dear God, please help me forgive myself and embrace the strange, estranged little girl who lives in me and is still afraid she may be the *bitch* Peter's teacher thought I was.

Who can refute the lie that I am a bitch better than me? Who can refute it but me? The whole world could be applauding, and I wouldn't be one iota happier or more secure—not for long anyway—unless and until *I* grasp my glory and own my greatness.

That sounds so pompous and arrogant to my ego-mind *I want to spit*, as my mother likes to say on the rare occasions when she gets really mad. But that fear of arrogance may be the very reason few of us dare come into our own. It feels way too risky. But I noticed something significant while I was crying those sweet tears over calling myself generous,

> A few years ago, I attended a workshop led by a friend's spiritual teacher, who surprised me by calling me a bitch out of the blue and in front of a large group. While he had no reason I could imagine to say that (I had said little), I felt ashamed and was upset for the rest of the weekend. I tried to ask him about it, but he refused to talk to me. It was pretty darned unpleasant, but his may have been the kick in the butt I needed to stop looking for teacher approval.
>
> ❧ ❧ ❧

funny, smart, quirky and interesting. I didn't feel in the least arrogant or better than anyone else for having said it.

Instead, I felt my head connected to my heart through a sincere appreciation of me at my best—who I honestly know myself to be. I felt connected, *period*. I was then, and am even now, far more united with myself, and so with our human family, than when I'm in my normal self-neutral or self-abnegating states. Since we are all one in the spirit, *wouldn't* we have to be in touch with our truest, loveliest nature—not as an idea in our heads, but as our fully felt experience—if we're to feel a part of, rather than apart from, the rest of the world? In order for me to see you and me as a wonderful *One*, I have to be deep in *wonderful oneness* myself. I've got to know I'm wonderful.

January 20, 2005

Longing for Recognition

Inauguration Day, God help us! I am still heartsick about the outcome of November's Presidential election. But it must be a measure of my growing detachment that I am far less activated than I was four years ago, when we first elected George W. Bush and I was practically inconsolable for weeks. Even as recently as six months ago, I burst into tears and wept for a good half an hour when I heard Ralph Nader had again entered the race and might spoil it for the Democrats.

Though it seems patently obvious to my ordinary mind, how do I know that wimpy Democrat John Kerry is better for this country than wimpy Republican George Bush? Kerry might have messed up less, but do I know for sure that survival of the human race is for the higher good? I can hardly figure out what's best for me. It has occurred to me that God may be practicing homeopathy, making things worse now as a means to making them better later, for God's sake if not the sake of us human beings. God knows we've screwed things up royally, and—it's the law of karma— actions have consequences, which continue to unfold at levels both cosmic and utterly personal.

If as I rediscovered yesterday I want to be recognized widely and well for the wise and wonderful woman I am, I must choose my actions with that consequence—*authentic* recognition—in mind. Knowing that should help me figure out what I do and don't want to do. Still, there is a question here. Yesterday when I asked myself what I want, an answer appeared at once. But was it *the* answer, the *right* answer, and who answered—my ego-mind or my heart? Both, I think.

I must recognize that *recognition* is what popped right out. I may wish that my heart's first desire is to be of service, or better yet perhaps, to attain enlightenment, but it seems not. Or maybe it is, and my heart's desire was overwhelmed by ego's more primary primal need to be seen and loved.

Or—and this is a leap for me—*maybe wanting recognition is a heartfelt aspiration after all.*

I am, let's face it, not made in the mold of Bapuji, a renunciate swami. I am a worldly American householder and glad to be. My most treasured yogic scripture *Sri Guru Gita* bears out that being in the world as I am is nothing to be ashamed of. "Life's enjoyments thou wilt attain" is one of its many lines promising material success to those who chant the *Gita* "with mind at peace." And to the surprise of those of us who have been taught that renunciation is The Way, Verse 144 says if you face east while chanting the *Gita*, you will "charm the hearts of men"—an attainment not, I'd say, all that far from the *recognition* I seek. The next verse goes further still:

> *By Gods and Kings thou wilt be adored;*
> *All God's creatures will honor thee.*
> *Of all the worlds thou wilt be the lord;*
> *From every bondage thou wilt be free.*

By Gods and Kings thou wilt be adored and All God's creatures will honor thee? Really?

Wow. I never thought about it that way before. But is this sacred scripture that has sustained me for decades suggesting that being *charming, adored* and *honored*— forms of my longed-for recognition, and then some—is a legitimate spiritual outcome of chanting its holy words? So it appears, since those three fruits are promised right along with the freedom from bondage assured us in the last line. If so, I am in luck. For whether you call it *recognition, honor* or *adoration*, we know *I* want some, and how good to know that I may not be entirely out of spiritual line in that persistent desire of mine. It may even make sense if you think how love works.

For if to give is to receive—and we know it is—to receive is also to give, particularly when it comes to love. When we are *in* love, we are neither giving nor receiving it. We can't be its donors or receptors only; if we are taking love in, we are also dishing it out, because we *are* it, and it is us. *In love*, we become the earthly conduits of the universal divine energy that sustains us all.

If we are taking love in, we are also dishing it out, because we are it.

We lovers are permeable vessels, love flowing to and through our open hearts all at once in an act we sometimes call grace. It doesn't work to ask for or grasp at love; we can only bask in it, as it beams into and right back out of us to other open hearts. Because true love is as impersonal as a ray of sun or a snowflake, we couldn't keep it to ourselves if we wanted to. The more recognized—the more *loved*—we feel, the more *love* we feel and *the more we have available and are bound to transmit.* If I am right about this, my desire for *recognition* may be nothing more or less than my heart's desire to be lost in love, with a dollop of healthy human ego thrown into the mix.

So what if my desire *is* partly ego-driven, which has been my fear? Ego is here to stay and we might as well keep him happy. Years ago I fretted to my friend Dennis about how something I wanted to do was being driven by ego. He suggested if I waited till ego was altogether out of

Ego is here to stay and we might as well keep him happy.

the way, I wouldn't do much. He was right, as he often is. False humility is one of ego's grand ploys, the other side of arrogance, both of them keeping us from playing as big as we are and need to be.

So let's go ahead and ask to be recognized widely and well, if we feel the urge. Let's learn to dive into and digest love and all true acknowledgment that comes to the wonderful people we most essentially are. Let's let ego take whatever bribes it may need to leave us alone and let us grow, and pass the remaining nourishment on through to the soul—our soul and the wide world of other souls we will be able to love if only we can love ourselves first. Being appreciated by you helps me appreciate me, which lets me dare share more love with you. Recognition be praised!

January 21, 2005

Resolutions about the Book

It's a beautiful cold winter's day, with time to write before a man arrives to clean our furnace, a noisy, disruptive affair. But I dallied, composing a needless email and taking too much time to clean up the kitchen and fuss with the fire. I am not sure why. Could it be the nostalgia—and its bedfellow inertia—that sets in in me, and Trond too, he tells me, as soon as hard winter arrives?

Though I felt refreshed when I stepped out earlier into sunlight glittering off frozen snow—the brightness mitigating the icy starkness of the winter landscape—it's different inside. Gazing at window-framed slivers of blue sky marked by bare brown branches, I fill with remembrance and longing. If April was T.S. Eliot's "cruelest month...mixing memory and desire," January is mine, bittersweet holiday recollections mingled with bits of hope for yet-unrealized resolutions.

Will this be the year I resolve my ten-year dilemma—*to write or not to write a book*? I am doing better than ever at trusting myself and the unfolding process. I have shown up every possible day in January to do this one thing in the direction of a book, demonstrating a new resolve I am grateful for. I am finally committed to finding words, or letting them find me, even if I still don't know quite what to do with them. But is there anything else I know to say about this? Maybe.

The writing coach duo I talked with recently asked me to define for myself what *I* know that is different from what other self-help writers offer. One thing I know that others may or may not is the power of *living organically*—letting life have me and me it, with as few rules or filters as I dare do without. What *I* know to do that may be different is to offer my forceful ego-mind in unfettered service to the heart and soul of me, through the human form that contains them both.

As well or better than most, I know how to slow down and listen, using my *body*'s unerring instincts and feelings to reveal what life has in mind for me. I give myself over into her wise hands (and heart!) with less resistance than ever before. It is this practice of coming back and back, in trust to my whole self—body, mind and spirit—one measured (or frantic) breath at a time that unfolds on these pages I fill. What I know to do that is different is to *do* almost nothing at all.

Now, as I breathe myself down from my head to my heart and listen in as I like to do, I know that yes, I want a book and not a blog. I know that no, I don't want to do preparatory exercises or market research, at least not yet. But yes, it would be good to begin typing up these handwritten journals or to find a way to get that done; but not at the expense of continuing to write—writing first, typing second (and only if *I* must). It might or might not be time to contact Maha's editor. We almost always know what we want. The bigger question is do we *want* to know what we want.

In the spirit of being willing to know what I know, I stay quiet, to discern if there is anything more than writing and typing I'd like to do about a book. Closing my eyes, I try to steady myself through breath.

We almost always know what we want. The bigger question is do we want to know what we want.

I feel mind wanting to jump in, take over and tell heart what to do, which leaves me tired and confused. So I'll stop writing and turn my full attention to hungry heart. May she get to have her say, and may I be still and receptive enough to hear her, as I now know how to do.

January 24, 2005

Dealing with Feelings I Hate

The weekend came and went, uneventful except for a huge chimney fire that could have burned the house down. Fortunately we were here Saturday night when the blaze began. Trond heard the chimney roaring and ran outside to check. Sure enough, flames were flaring out of the top like wildfire. Trond being Trond, which is to say competent to a fault, managed to put the fire out.

It wasn't easy. And we spent the next many hours vacuuming, dusting and mopping up the considerable mess made by smoke, ashes and spray from the fire extinguisher. The effects were horribly apparent in our lovely living room and beyond. Did I say the weekend was uneventful?

Even before the fire, and for most of the weekend afterward, I felt out of sorts. It started Friday when I let myself get crazy-frustrated about another Blue Cross coverage denial, a huge air miles attribution oversight, and a downed fax machine, among other petty annoyances. I lost it and still haven't found it, *it* being the elusive center where I am always okay, and love lives, no matter what I do or don't do, no matter what happens around me. Yes, fear has gotten a toehold again.

I am afraid that I can't write a book, that I am wasting my life, and that I must be fooling myself to imagine people could take interest in or benefit from what feels today like my piddling journey. It's a nasty, nagging feeling, this frightened ego-soaked unworthiness, which feeds the equally burning, churning desire for recognition.

While I would do well to take my own advice—that in order to let unwelcome feelings go, we must let them come—I am loathe to sit in the shit again.

In order to let unwelcome feelings go, we must let them come.

If there's another way, I don't know it. Or maybe I do, since it just occurred to me prayer might help. *Dear God, please let me be present and still. Let me make sacred space for this queasy, disquieted part of me welling up from my turgid depths, pretending most convincingly to be the real Suzanne Grenager. Let me welcome but not wallow in the egoic part of me that eschews silence and self-acceptance, and would make any noise or disturbance just to get noticed.*

How to welcome the unwelcome within? We know that I know. Put down the pen, Suzanne, close the journal and your eyes, and feel how you feel, *simply feel it*…. I do, and what do I find? I find if I give something as ephemeral as a feeling my patient, patent attention—poof! Now you see it, now you don't. There is nothing to it. *Let it be*, and *this too shall pass*, the one cliché leading right to the other. When we attend wholeheartedly to what is, however unpleasant it starts out being, we (be)come present, and the power of presence takes precedence over everything else.

When I make the strangely difficult choice to be fully here in body, mind and spirit, the object of my awareness, and my sense of the pain or pleasure it causes, ceases to matter. I am able to get happily lost in the spaciousness of mind's expanding inner *I*. Today, writing well eludes me, or so I think. But *so what*, ye of little faith? There's always tomorrow, until one day, there isn't.

January 25, 2005

Bapuji and Me on Struggle
and Self-Observation

It's another day, another blank page, but quite another
Suzanne. Far from yesterday's mute despair, today finds *me*
blank, open and ripe for inspired self-expression of the verbal
variety. Thank God—and my willingness to take the advice I
gave Liz and another of yesterday's clients, the two of them by
their accounts as messed up emotionally as I was: be patient
with yourself, *especially* when you are a mess and feel least
like it. And so I was—both messed up *and* patient.

Some days words wonderfully pave the way down into
the heart of me. Other days, like yesterday, words seem to
raise a shield against emotions' onslaught, keeping me from
feeling and moving through the pain to my truest self. Then
it's best to put down the pen and leave myself defenseless,
which is what I did. Letting go yesterday worked to a point,
prayer and attention bringing at least a brief respite from the
sense of fearful inadequacy that prevailed for much of the rest
of the day.

Does this *ever* happen to Katie or my friend Jim, both of
whom claim full enlightenment? I don't know because they
don't write about it. Katie helps others transform by leading
them through the step-by-step process of her Work and says
little about herself. Jim, who has been handicapped lately by
strokes—God bless him—writes like Tolle from the other side
of the "enlightenment line," pointing seekers to the illumined
experience we seek. "Drop your story," he counsels, insisting
that our story (whatever it is) fuels the illusion that we are as

we seem. Feeling as he does about stories, Jim says little about *his* story or any struggles he may have faced.

Years ago, Jim had suggested to me that I too should write from a fully enlightened perspective, as if I were already there even when I feel I am not. At the time, I paid strict attention to what writers and teachers I admired had to say about what I could or should be writing. Since I was telling

> Though Jim Dreaver used to write from a fairly philosophical perspective, his writing has become increasingly personal and, I think, all the more compelling for it.
>
> ❧ ❧ ❧

my far-from-enlightened stories regularly in a column for SpiritSite.com, Jim's advice to avoid storytelling threw me into quite the little spin. Maybe he's right, I recall thinking. Maybe I am keeping readers mired in their made-up muck by inviting them to wade around with me in mine.

Little by little I've grown in confidence about the value of sharing my story, and of its likely relevance to a larger world. I can say for practically certain that most of us who have woken up to the dream that is everyday life are not on a fast track to God. Ours can be a slow, circuitous and arduous path from ignorance to bliss. Many people I know who are leaning into the light wrestle daily with darkness. Sharing our experiences—our *stories*—of battling our demons *and making our progress* reminds us we are not alone in our struggles, even if our way must be ours alone.

So yes, this is a *story*—of one woman coming into her gory glory. It's a story of pain and fear, but also I now understand, of comfort and hope. It says we are not crazy to be hurting, and hey, if I can do it—this way today, that way tomorrow—so, beloved reader, can you. We are in the soup together, and by holding hands and joining hearts, we can work ourselves out into the clear air.

Just watch. I do it for you and you do it for me, one spicy, dicey wheeling-dealing moment at a time. This story of mine is one small piece of the action, and God willing, it will continue in books to come. Take it or leave it. But if it helps, why *not* take it, take *me*, and *use me for all I am worth.*

What on earth else is there to do but hold each other close and tell it like it is, as we claw our way toward radiance? If it's Jim's and Tolle's job to describe transcendence, and Katie's to help us manage our judging minds, it is mine to document the descents and dissensions that make up the precipitous

What on earth else is there to do but hold each other close and tell it like it is, as we claw our way toward radiance?

ascent—with our holy human bodies (heart, guts and all) the beacons lighting our way.

To be of utmost service, we must live loud and each shout out what we're learning, though it may be in our own quiet way. With the exception of one long-ago miraculous day, my experience has rarely been of steady light. Far more often, my journey takes me into the bowels of my being— from whence dark dissidents would run me, unless and until I gently or (on bad days) rudely rout them out. That is what I have been doing, so that is all I have to share. You'll get no twelve steps, four questions or seven laws from me (useful as those might sometimes be).

Mine is dirty, undistinguished work, little polished, clean or by-the-numbers about it. If we are to get free of what isn't love, we've got to drop the numbers, especially the ones we do on ourselves. And we've got to stop looking for someone else's magic bullet. There is nothing for it but to come clean *our* way, being willing to feel and fell the fear that stops us, one full-bodied bout at a time.

There is nothing for it but to come clean our way, being willing to feel and fell the fear that stops us, one full-bodied bout at a time.

Though we know there's no one way for everybody, telling our individual war stories helps. If we want to know love, we've got to mess in and unmask the unlovely muck that surrounds it. We must hold the torch high and hack through the jungle of no-love with our machete pens—or whatever our particular arsenal of self-expression gives us to work with—firmly in hand.

If it were so easy to be free, wouldn't more people be enlightened? No less a saint than Bapuji seems to understand our difficulties in that struggle talk I keep coming back to. "All life is struggle…life means struggle…so anyone born into this world must be a warrior," is how it begins. "Man lives in constant pain. And so life means endless pain and endless remedy." Indeed!

But what to do about it? How can we make progress in the face of endless pain, struggle, and attempted remedies? Elsewhere in my battered book of Bapuji talks lies an answer. The best we can do, he suggests, is to *pay close attention to pain and remedies alike.* Even though I didn't know it until recently, I must have been paying close attention to what he said. For watching the self with fierce honesty *and compassion* is precisely what I have been trying to do, and teaching my yoga students and coaching clients to do, as best I can. Isn't that what this story is about?

"Self analysis and self-observation are the key to

progress on the spiritual path," according to my late great
master teacher. "But," Bapuji warns us gently, "you cannot
come to accurate self-observation and analysis immediately.
It is a gradual process (all italics in quotes from his talks are
mine) and in the beginning you will have to accept the fact
that *there will be faults in your self-observation*," he adds
by way of encouragement I'm sure, as encouragement was
always his way.

"When you are able to observe everything that happens
in your life with keen awareness, like a scientist," he
continues, "and draw inspiration from each action, then you
will really be able to grow" (and to experience less pain, says
I). How marvelous that Bapuji understood self-scrutiny is a
process, which may take our whole life to hone. He seems to
be talking about himself too!

"You must constantly check the storehouse of your
knowledge," he kindly instructs us, "asking yourself whether
you have increased it over what you had before. Then check
the storehouse of your actions: *have you really given up those
actions that produce suffering, and are you performing only
those actions that will bring you true happiness and peace?*
Next, check the storehouse of your love," says the greatest
lover I ever knew, "and *see if your love for God has increased
even a little bit.*" What sure guidance. How I love his words,
so sweet and true.

The path Bapuji describes and prescribes for us, which
surely flowed from his experience—how else would he
know?—is by his own account a slow, challenging one. We
must watch ourselves living our lives and we must watch,
in his words, "with peace of mind, complete honesty and
objectivity." This has to be a painful process, since if we
are truly honest with ourselves, we will not always like

what we see. And that is likely to shake our objectivity and peace of mind.

Blaming ourselves for behaving in a way that creates suffering only creates more suffering. So if we are to grow, we must look at ourselves—body, mind and spirit—with clear-eyed *kindhearted* awareness. We must try to see how our thoughts, words and deeds do and don't work to promote peace and love, for ourselves and others. We must adjust ourselves accordingly, in each moment

Blaming ourselves for behaving in a way that creates suffering only creates more suffering.

and over a lifetime. In this self-nurturing way, our storehouse of love, for ourselves and for God—and for ourselves as God—is bound to grow. *But it is a journey for a warrior, and nothing less.*

I am that warrior, daughter of a guru, and granddaughter of a master. I pray this brightening winter morning that I might be strong and valiant enough to stand with legions in the painful battle which, as Bapuji has shown us in his heroic life and death, can at last be won. These remarkable closing words in the talk "On Life and Struggle" must stem from his own hard-won knowledge:

"When the yogi at last wins the great struggle, he experiences indescribable bliss. He looks around him and sees Almighty God standing right beside him. He embraces God and then he remembers something. He turns around and pranams (bows down) again and again to a defeated struggle left behind him and prays to it with a pure heart: O great benefactor! Creator of my destiny! I have so often turned you away, but you have ignored my ill will and placed me at the feet of Almighty God. Without your help, true humanity and divinity are difficult to obtain. *Angels of struggle, let your victory be everywhere.*"

To share my struggles that others may know theirs as the holy rites of passage they are; that is my mission and my heart's desire. May my will to serve grow strong enough to draw me along my path. May the struggle cease. No, no. That's not right. Rather, *may I accept these ceaseless struggles as an inherent part of the way, and surrender to them with all the love I can muster.*

Bapuji, who became extremely gaunt and pained-looking during his last year among us, must have known whereof he spoke when he said, "Man lives in constant pain." As I struggle with the sharp pain that seems to have settled into the back of my head for the long haul—and the omnipresent myriad aches often plaguing the rest of me (body, mind and spirit)—may the love that overcame Bapuji please fill me to overflowing. May today be a day of sweet acceptance, and may God Almighty bless us all in our struggles and in our overcoming of them.

> Toward the end of his stay in America, **Bapuji**, who had been robust in body and spirit when he arrived in 1977, was failing from what appeared to be cancer. Because he refused Amrit's entreaties to see a physician, we will never know. But after four-and-a-quarter years here, he returned to India in 1981 to die. His body was wasted but his spirit was very much alive the day he wished his spiritual grandchildren farewell. Here is what he said to us, in part: "Beloved children, do not give up virtuous conduct and self-discipline, even in the face of death. Keep unflinching faith in the holy lotus feet of the Lord. I extend my blessing to everyone."
>
> ❧ ❧ ❧

Postscript

Though *this* book has ended, my story is far from over and the beat goes insistently on. The strong, sometimes outrageous voice filling the pages of *Bare Naked at the Reality Dance* has continued to offer itself—if anything, with greater force and clarity—whenever I have been brave and still enough to let her rip. Because I want you to grasp for *your* life the daring one-of-a-kind ride it is to become your full-blown self, I plan to share more of my odyssey with you. The point I mean to make is always this: *There is nothing wrong with us and if I can do it, so can you.*

Since I am in an aging mortal body prone to aches, pains and off-the-wall emotions, you'll find me still doubting and struggling in books to come. But so what? I don't expect the struggle to end till the fat lady sings and I'm within spitting distance of the light at the end of the tunnel. So you won't see me getting bopped over the head with an enlightenment wand—not any time soon.

What you will see is me getting more comfortable in my skin—better at seeing and being myself in ways that make a radical difference, to me, those around me, and I hope humanity at large. That focus on *self-realization* may be the hardest thing in the world to do. But it's also the only thing in the world worth doing, for ourselves and for the world. So when I choose to remember, that is what I do, and by example, what I urge you to do, as we work the spiritual trenches together.

Thanks to some shocking prods from my life coach Maha in the next book, you'll watch the fire of my transformation and its freedom sparks burn hotter. Maha is followed by a crew of other rousing women who show up and *force me to show up*—as my (still occasionally terrified) fully authentic self. The last few years have presented me with exhilarating new opportunities to face down my lingering codependence, pride and a host of other fear-driven ghosts, while I have been boldly (and I trust ever more humbly) stepping into the love that I am and we all essentially are.

Along the way, I get exposed—and almost magically called—to a feminine style of leadership, rife with a fiery, fulfilling co-creativity unknown to Amrit and Ilana, and it's a part of the story that's forever changed my life. Meanwhile, it is in that spirit of warm, generous and passionate collaboration that my life work has continued to unfold. I don't yet know what's next and I don't need to know. I do know, though, that we are all part of a sweet, awfully mysterious equation.

For ours is a common universal story of unfolding struggle, which Bapuji, the most joyous person I've known, reminds us is not only life's bloody lot, but the source of our salvation. Struggle, he has gently told us, is the creator of our destiny, the benefactor that brings us at last to the feet of Almighty God—and, I might add, to stand on our own two feet. Because we are all one in the spirit, my struggle is your struggle, and my overcoming of struggle is also your overcoming.

So won't you please join me in doing whatever it takes to turn ourselves and the stuff of our lives away from fear and doubt, and back to our incandescent essence—*love*—which alone will save us. May we together become the host of embodied lovers that this world now most desperately needs.

It is my privilege and joy to have walked this far with you and I hope to see you again!

Acknowledgments

Only after my handwritten words were typed did I discover that my grand-guru Swami Kripalvananda was the inspiration for *Bare Naked at the Reality Dance*. I was astonished to find Bapuji's sweet traces throughout the manuscript and don't quite know how he got there. I had known, of course, that he mattered in my life, but I had no idea how deeply he had ingrained himself in my being. I bow down in a gratitude beyond words for the love, service, surrender—and consummate good humor—he made flesh, showing us what is possible in human form. I am extremely grateful, too, to his close disciple, my early yoga teacher and later guru, Amrit Desai, for his powerful teachings.

These two yoga masters set my soul on fire, paving a spiritual way that became my own. Bapuji embodied love. But it was Amrit who first introduced me to the transformative energy of Shakti as a potent palpable force, throwing me out of my willful head and opening me to the love center at my core. And it was Amrit who memorably said *the body is a gross mind and the mind a subtle body,* a compelling truth that set me on the path of urgent self-exploration that continues to this day.

I am thankful, too, to Ilana Rubenfeld, founder of the Rubenfeld Synergy Method. Her seminal work, using the body as a graceful gateway to the soul, helped me grasp the meaning of Amrit's words and apply it to managing—and surrendering into—the messy, marvelous business of my life. Their combined wisdom helped me realize that body is both temple *and* template of the spirit, and that to hearken to its down-to-earth sensuality and off-the-wall feelings is to tune to the songs of our soul.

It was two very different people who encouraged me to craft a first book from the words Bapuji and Amrit inspired. My friend Carol Keller was so inflamed and changed by typing up what I'd written that I knew I had to do something significant with it. But more than anyone else, it is Trond, my ever supportive, loving husband—my forty-year mainstay in all ways—who became the tireless keeper of the publishing flame. Trond has been my editor, my gentle taskmaster, my assistant and cheerleader, from the first days of journaling the words until this very moment. Without Carol's transformation and Trond's constancy, I would not have had the guts to show up bare naked at this reality dance.

I am thankful for my inspiring coaching clients and others who appear in the book, many of whose names were changed to protect their privacy. A generous handful of women encouraged and actively supported the several year odyssey to birthing *Bare Naked at the Reality Dance*—notably my life coaches Maha and Kimberly, and my friends Mary Fowke and Karen Latvala, both early enthusiastic readers whose suggestions made the book better. Laine Cunningham, my editorial reviewer, offered a framework for shaping the initially unwieldy journal entries and saw the value I wasn't yet sure about.

From start to finish, Bethany Brown and Amy Collins of The Cadence Group have been unfailingly generous and smart in sharing their extensive knowledge of all things publishing and marketing. I could not have done it without them. And Maggie Lichtenberg, with her insider experience in the traditional publishing world, was very helpful in

banishing the devil from the myriad troubling details a
self-publishing author must face. Along with Trond, Lynne
Cosby, my editor, friend and ally, deserves supreme thanks
for the finished product. Her skill and great dedication
to patiently polishing the words have made them and my
message shine.

My heartfelt appreciation goes to Shannon Bodie for
her stunning cover and elegant interior design, the enticing
icing on the cake. Thanks to my friend Jim Dreaver, who has
long encouraged my writing and offered to look at the book
and write the first endorsement. I am grateful to the Kripalu
Center for Yoga & Health for its gracious permission to
quote extensively from Bapuji's teachings.

I offer verbal bouquets to Natalie Goldberg and Anne
Lamott for their groundbreaking books about writing.
Their distinctive feminine voices helped me find and trust
my own. Many other authors—particularly Byron Katie
and Eckhart Tolle—have inspired and informed me, and
countless friends have believed in me. To all of you I shout
out a sonorous THANK YOU. If it takes a village to raise a
child, it takes a den of literary lions to birth a book without
a publishing house. Together we did it!

About the Author

Suzanne Selby Grenager grew up in the Philadelphia suburbs and attended The Baldwin School. She went on to Mount Holyoke and Barnard Colleges and taught at the Woodstock School in the Indian Himalayas before being selected as the NBC Scholar at the University of Pennsylvania's Annenberg School for Communication. Following stints as an actress, advertising copywriter, education publicist and publications director, she became an education columnist for the *Philadelphia Inquirer*. An early advocate of job-sharing for mothers, she herself shared two positions.

The grim death of her best friend in 1975 radically changed Suzanne's focus, kick-starting a lifelong love affair with the Inner Self she hadn't paid attention to till then. She began using the powerful tools of Kripalu Yoga to get out of her driven mind and deep into her heart, soul and guts. For two decades she was an eager yoga student and teacher to thousands, at Dickinson College and throughout Central Pennsylvania. Ten of those years she served as Kripalu Network Mid-Atlantic regional leader, for which she was honored with a 1994 Global Service Award for exemplary leadership.

Suzanne's yearning to help people turn their fears back to source love led to certification and a subsequent practice in the ground-breaking body-mind-spirit Rubenfeld Synergy Method. In 1999, she began training with the Coaches Training Institute and became a life coach and spiritual mentor. She has written for *Yoga Journal* and was a columnist for Spiritsite.com.

Suzanne lives with her husband Trond, a Norwegian architect, on a Pennsylvania farm where they raised their two children, Teg and Nora, myriad animals, and gardens of organic vegetables. They spent a year in Egypt and later started a pioneering business turning garbage gas into electric power for Metropolitan Edison. They also own and operate a traditional boatyard in Nova Scotia, which is their second home. For more about Suzanne, this book and the ones to come, as well as for her current blog writing, please visit www.suzannegrenager.com.

CPSIA information can be obtained at www.ICGtesting.com
Printed in the USA
BVOW031853301112

306853BV00003B/14/P